W9-BOL-654

Beyond Budgeting

In the cases we researched for this book, we detected several indepen-
dent strands of management philosophy that have contributed much to
the development of the beyond budgeting model. Of these, our greatest
source of inspiration has been the philosophy of radical decentralization
as exemplified at Svenska Handelsbanken. In a period of crisis, then-
Chairman Tore Browaldh appointed Jan Wallander as Chief Executive
in 1970. Wallander became the visionary architect of the management
model Handelsbanken uses today. One of his first and most decisive acts
was to abandon budgeting and the bureaucracy it supports. It took his
strong determination, persuasion, and enthusiasm to bring about these
changes. His experience over forty years provides strong evidence that
the principles and practices we describe in this book will provide a solid
foundation for sustainable improvement.

Beyond Budgeting

**How Managers Can Break Free
from the Annual Performance Trap**

Jeremy Hope

Robin Fraser

HARVARD BUSINESS SCHOOL PRESS

Boston, Massachusetts

This book is dedicated to our families
whose support made it possible.

Dot, Ben, Vicky, and Oliver

and

Farideh, Mariam, and Anna

Copyright 2003 Harvard Business School Publishing Corporation

All rights reserved

Printed in the United States of America

18 17 16 15 14

No part of this publication may be reproduced, stored in or introduced into a retrieval system, or transmitted, in any form, or by any means (electronic, mechanical, photocopying, recording, or otherwise), without the prior permission of the publisher. Requests for permission should be directed to permissions@hbsp.harvard.edu, or mailed to Permissions, Harvard Business School Publishing, 60 Harvard Way, Boston, Massachusetts 02163.

978-1-57851-866-1 (ISBN 13)
Library of Congress Cataloging-in-Publication Data

Hope, Jeremy.
    Beyond budgeting : how managers can break free from the annual performance trap / Jeremy Hope and Robin Fraser.
        p. cm.
    Includes bibliographical references and index.
    ISBN 1-57851-866-0 (alk. paper)
        1. Management. 2. Fraser, Robin, 1941–   II. Title.
    HD31 .H635 2003
    658—dc21

                                                                2002015622

The paper used in this publication meets the requirements of the American National Standard for Permanence of Paper for Publications and Documents in Libraries and Archives Z39.48-1992.

Frontispiece: Tore Browaldh (left), Chairman, and Dr. Jan Wallander (right), CEO, Svenska Handelsbanken. Painted in 1977 by John-Erik Franzén, Member of the Royal Swedish Academy of Fine Arts.

Contents

Part IV   Realizing the Full Promise of Beyond Budgeting

Foreword

Beyond Budgeting may be a provocative title for a book. But do not be misled. This book focuses on the whole general management model, not just the replacement of time-worn, badly managed budgeting processes. Beyond budgeting is not merely a negative idea that trashes budgeting. Instead, it is a positive idea that uses the abandonment of budgeting as a trigger for improving the entire management control process. Budget abandonment forces deeper and broader examination of how organizations should be managed.

Budgeting is at the heart of how nearly all large corporations in the world are managed today. Managers are deeply dissatisfied with it, but few have really challenged budgeting. This book does. It describes an alternative coherent management model tailored to today's business conditions. It overcomes many of the limitations of the traditional management model. This is not a cookbook. There is no package solution. However, this book provides a guiding framework for how organizations should be managed in the twenty-first century.

How should we view this in the United States? Our way of managing organizations has been the dominant model throughout the past century. It has been copied around the world. As conditions have changed, we have recognized its weaknesses. And we have developed useful tools and techniques such as activity-based costing and the Balanced Scorecard to deal with them. But have they really worked? Have they fundamentally changed anything? Could they have worked better within a different management model? Is there really such an alternative model? Or is it just more hype?

This book addresses these questions. Be clear that beyond budgeting is not just another tool. This book offers an alternative general management model. It will make many managers uneasy because it takes us beyond our functional comfort zones. It forces us to recognize the interdependence of the whole management process. This means changing not only how goals are set but also how reward systems must be re-aligned. It also forces us to think about whether management processes and the behavior they spur produce the outcomes we want. This res-onates with many in the aftermath of a number of high-profile cases of inadequate corporate governance and unethical accounting practices.

The authors base their thesis on a rich variety of cases. But imple-menting it will not be easy—especially in the United States. Our culture celebrates winners and admires heroic leaders. We foster individualism. We believe in tough targets and high rewards. We bind managers to aggressive performance contracts. And we are control oriented. But are these cultural ingredients right for these times?

Recent events have shown that there has never been a better time for a radical reassessment of how we manage organizations. We face rapid change despite having more limited sight than at any time since the 1940s. A climate of international terrorism and volatile stock markets does not encourage planning beyond weeks and months, never mind months and years. We need more adaptive processes and a culture that supports them. Instead, too often we have fixed targets and fixed plans. They no longer make sense. Beyond budgeting is a provoking alternative we should take seriously.

Who will benefit from reading this book? The word *budgeting* in its title might suggest that it aims at finance staff. But this would be a mis-take. The authors address much more than financial management pro-cesses. Finance managers can be key in transforming the general man-agement model. They are the guardians of most of its processes. They can be persuasive advocates for change and can be critical to the change project. But they cannot do it alone. To implement the model success-fully, the CEO and his or her top team must understand it, buy into it, truly believe in it, and actively lead and support it.

Managers in all organizations should get value from reading this book. Management consultants will gain a broader perspective of the context within which particular initiatives may be introduced. Consul-tants will see more clearly how the coherence of the management model as a whole can support or conflict with their favorite ideas and tools. IT vendors will see how the effectiveness of their software solutions can be increased. Accounting professors may see in this book many areas for new research. They may also wish to use the book to help their students to think about the implications of beyond budgeting for their future careers as finance professionals.

Most of the solutions generally proposed for management problems involve putting something new into the organization. In this regard, beyond budgeting is very different. Perhaps uniquely, it proposes taking something powerful out to make room for something new and even more powerful. We have all the tools and techniques we need. What we lack is the right overall context for them to work effectively. This book provides a vision for that context.

Charles T. Horngren
Littlefield Professor of Accounting, Emeritus,
Stanford University

Acknowledgments

This book is the result of an unusual process of case-based research and shared learning that has extended over a five-year period. It has involved a huge number and wide variety of participants. We explain the process here, identifying the participants and their particular contribution to the development of "beyond budgeting."

We had long held the view that budgeting is fundamentally flawed. We believed that in today's conditions the solution was not better budgeting, but rather abandoning budgeting entirely and building an alternative management model. Few shared our view. Fewer still were prepared to fund serious research into it. However, our prospects changed when we heard through Pertti Akerburg, then group controller at Valmet in Finland, that there were companies that had actually abandoned budgeting. Several of them were in Sweden, and one of these had worked without budgets for thirty years. His news proved to be the stimulus we needed.

Accordingly, in late 1997 we set up the Beyond Budgeting Round Table (BBRT) with CAM-I, an international research consortium. Thirty-three companies joined us in 1998 to find out how companies had replaced budgeting and whether this alternative model was really different (and better). Since then over sixty companies in total have joined the BBRT and funded our research. Their interest stemmed from their own experience—growing dissatisfaction, indeed frustration, with traditional budgeting. They have traveled this journey with us, shared in the learning process, and challenged our thinking at every stage.

Although the BBRT's origins are in the United Kingdom, members have joined us from many countries, including Belgium, France, Germany, Holland, Norway, South Africa, Sweden, Switzerland, the United Kingdom, and the United States. We thank particularly the BBRT chairmen: Mark Doyle of Diageo, Martyn Newlands of Cadbury Schweppes, and Steve Morlidge of Unilever. Their guidance has been invaluable.

We also thank the representatives and participants from all the member companies. We are privileged to have worked with so many fine organizations: ABB, ABC Technologies, Accenture, ACCO Europe, AC Nielsen, Adaytum, Alstom Energy, Anheuser Busch, Armstrong-Laing, Arthur Andersen, Ascom, Barclays Bank, Bass Brewers, BG Transco, Boots, British Telecom, Bulmers, Burmah Castrol, Cadbury Schweppes, Chartered Institute of Management Accountants, De Beers, Deutsche Bank, DHL, Diageo, Droitwich Spa and Rural Housing Association, eNiklas, Ernst & Young, European Bank (EBRD), Halifax, Hammond Suddards, Interbrew, Kingfisher, KPMG Consulting, Mars, Mencap, National Power, Navigant Consulting, Novartis, Parker Hannifin, Pentland Group, Port of Tyne Authority, PricewaterhouseCoopers, ProDaCapo, Royal Mail, Rugby Group, Sainsburys, Schneider Electric, Siemens, Sight Savers International, SKF, Southco, Standard Life, TPG (TNT), Texas Instruments, Thames Water, UBS, Unilever, United Engineering Forgings, Valmet Corporation, West Bromwich Building Society, and Whitbread.

The cases we chose to visit initially were companies that had abandoned or radically changed their planning, budgeting, and control processes. But as the study progressed we widened our criteria. We included, for example, some companies that were decentralized, some that had implemented unusual reward systems, and some that used budgets differently (even one that believed it used budgets effectively!). In each case we sought a range of opinions from managers at different levels, from CEO to unit supervisor, as well as from different functions and locations.

We focused our research on three questions: (1) Is there an alternative to budgeting? (2) Is there a better management model? (3) What lessons can we learn about implementation? In total we visited some twenty cases (several on more than one occasion), wrote reports about them for the BBRT members, received presentations at BBRT meetings from executives of the case companies, and discussed the cases with them.

As our journey continued we identified common principles from these case reports, and we gradually built and refined what has since become known as the beyond budgeting model. We tested our thinking with the members of the BBRT, the executives in our cases, and also a range of academics and other experts who joined our meetings.

In addition to this, we produced a guide to managing without budgets. We prepared a Web-based diagnostic that any company can use (http://www.project.bbrt.org). We undertook an exploratory survey on over two hundred companies to test for correlation between progress toward the beyond budgeting model and improved competitive performance (it was statistically significant). And we have explored the use of a range of recognized tools and systems within the model. This book draws on this work and tells our story through the participants. In particular, these include the people we interviewed on case visits and the presenters at our meetings. It is because we could not have written the book without them that we have let them do much of the talking.

The cases have been our main source of new learning and inspiration. The companies at which we conducted interviews included AES, Ahlsell, Boots, Borealis, Bulmers, CIBA Vision, Bull, Fokus Bank, Leyland Trucks, Rhodia, Sight Savers International, SKF, Sprint, Svenska Handelsbanken, and Volvo Cars. Most of these case visits took place in the period from 1998 to 2001. We interviewed many people on each visit, too many to name individually. We thank them all, but would like to acknowledge especially the contribution of Gunnar Haglund at Ahlsell, Bjarte Bogsnes and Thomas Boesen at Borealis, Lesley Jackson at Bulmers, Richard Peach and Marco Caron at Novartis/Ciba Vision, Terje Svendsen at Fokus Bank, Charlie Poskett at Leyland Trucks, Jacky Pinçon at Rhodia, Adrian Poffley at Sight Savers International, and Arne Mårtensson and Sven Grevelius at Svenska Handelsbanken. They have all enriched and enlivened our project and our knowledge in equal measure.

However, behind each of our cases lies a philosophy. Our real aim in visiting them was to understand it. We detected several independent strands that have contributed much to the development of the beyond budgeting model. The philosophy behind the remarkable turnarounds at both Bull and CarnaudMetalbox in France, for example, is that of Jean-Marie Descarpentries. But our greatest inspiration for beyond budgeting has been the philosophy of radical decentralization of Dr. Jan Wallander, honorary chairman at Svenska Handelsbanken.

In 1970, as the then recently appointed CEO, Dr. Wallander abandoned the budgeting and central planning systems and became the visionary architect of the management model Handelsbanken uses today. It took his strong determination, persuasion, and enthusiasm (clearly visible in the figure at the very front of the book) to bring about these changes in the bank. His experience over forty years provides strong evidence that the principles and practices we describe will not just sparkle today and fizzle tomorrow.

Many others have also contributed to the development of *Beyond Budgeting*. We thank particularly our academic advisers: Professors Michael Bromwich at the London School of Economics, Charles Horngren at Stanford University, Michel Lebas at the HEC in Paris, David Ottley at Lancaster School of Management, and Andy Neely at Cranfield University. Others also have been very generous with their time in presenting to the BBRT at its meetings. These include Dr. Stephan Haeckel, Professor Robert Kaplan, Dr. David Norton, and many others.

This book, like any major piece of work, is a team effort. It could not have been written without the help and support of a number of people within the BBRT. We would especially like to thank Woody Noxon, Dr. Peter Bunce, Pamela Sweetnam, Carol Carter, and Christine Jackson, who have supported our efforts over an extended period. The BBRT (see http://www.bbrt.org for more details) has now begun to spread into other regions beyond Europe. There are now sister BBRTs in North America and Australasia. We thank their leaders, Steve Player in the United States and John Bragg in Australia, for their support.

Finally, we would also like to thank our editors at the Harvard Business School Press. Jacque Murphy, Lindsay Whitman, and Jill Connor have shown patience and perseverance as we have battled to turn the concepts of beyond budgeting into a relevant and practical manifesto for change.

Introduction: Toward a New General Management Model

> The budget is a tool of repression rather than innovation.[1]
> —BOB LUTZ, EX-CEO, CHRYSLER

> Budgeting is an unnecessary evil.
> —DR. JAN WALLANDER, HONORARY PRESIDENT,
> SVENSKA HANDELSBANKEN

> The budget is the bane of corporate America.[2]
> —JACK WELCH, EX-CEO, GENERAL ELECTRIC

Every business leader wants competitive success, the best management team, continuous innovation, low costs, loyal customers, and high standards of corporate governance and control. But for most, these goals remain pipe dreams. And despite spending huge sums on enterprisewide information systems and a range of tools such as the Balanced Scorecard, they appear to be just as far away as ever. Some might point to the pursuit of ineffective strategies. Though there have been many strategic mistakes (especially in the high-tech and telecom markets), there have also been plenty of excellent examples of imaginative and well-crafted strategies. The failure is, by and large, not one of strategy. It is a failure of execution.

The problem is that the management model used by most organizations today is not up to the job. It was designed to enable leaders to plan and control their organizations from the center. Enabling business units and subunits throughout the organization to focus on creating value for customers and shareholders was never part of its design. But that is what it is being asked to do. The Balanced Scorecard has provided a strategic framework to help overcome some of these problems, but most scorecards still play second fiddle to a core management process driven by the annual budgeting cycle.

The budgeting process has much to answer for. That it is too long, too expensive, and adds little value is not in doubt. Nor do most managers need much convincing that it is out of kilter with the competitive environment. But it has even more insidious effects that are perhaps less obvious.

Budgets (or any planning and measurement frameworks, for that matter) don't exist in a vacuum. They determine how people behave in any given situation. Focusing leaders' minds on the stewardship of shareholders' funds and ensuring that managers worried about controlling costs were its original functions, and leaders and managers, by and large, behaved accordingly. But budgets have since been hijacked by a generation of financial engineers that have used them as remote control devices to "manage by the numbers." They have turned budgets into *fixed performance contracts* that force managers at all levels to commit to delivering specified financial outcomes, even though many of the variables underpinning those outcomes are beyond their control. This leads to undesirable and, in many cases, unethical behavior.

One large survey of U.S. companies concluded that managers either did not accept the budgetary targets and opted to beat the system or felt pressured to achieve the targets at any cost.[3] This pressure is squeezing the life and spirit out of many organizations and their people. It's the mentality that says, "Do what I say or your future is at risk." It is driven by greed and a need for instant gratification and immediate results. These problems also occur at the highest level. The torrent of media criticism about how firms have been "managing their earnings" (especially following the Enron and WorldCom scandals) has highlighted the behavioral consequences of these links.

Budgets provide poor value. They fail to address current competitive imperatives. And they lead to dysfunctional behavior. It is perhaps little wonder that an increasing number of large organizations are attracted by the idea of breaking free from this budget-induced annual performance trap. They want to learn from organizations that have already escaped to find out what alternatives are available.

They will find plenty of exemplars. We have visited and reported upon many of them over recent years. They range across industries, countries, and cultures. In some cases the initiatives have come from new leaders with a mandate for visionary change. In others, they have come from enthusiastic senior managers (typically finance professionals) who have to persuade their colleagues of the case for change. In most cases they learned by their mistakes. Though these were, by and large, unconnected cases, we were able to piece together a common set of processes and principles to guide prospective followers (though their application varied considerably).

Beyond Budgeting is not a toolset designed to fix a specific problem with budgets or anything else. Nor is it a set of processes that can be cherry-picked to suit the requirements of senior managers who claim to have identified particular weaknesses in their information systems. Plastering over the cracks of the existing management model based on central control is not its purpose. Rather, it offers an alternative management model based on the decision-making needs of front-line managers. It is a coherent set of alternative processes that support relative targets and rewards, continuous planning, resources on demand, dynamic cross-company coordination, and a rich array of multilevel controls. None of this means loosening performance standards. The effects are just the opposite. Performance responsibility is transferred from the center to business units and, in more mature cases, to the front line. The heightened sense of ownership and commitment that comes from involving local people in setting goals and actions provides the driving force for continuous improvement.

This book has four parts. Part I is about breaking free from the annual performance trap. Chapter 1 explains how this trap is sprung whenever managers are pressured to meet fixed targets by fixed dates. Chapter 2 provides an overview of the two opportunities of beyond budgeting.

Part II, which deals with the first opportunity, is about how a number of organizations have used beyond budgeting principles to implement more adaptive processes. In place of fixed performance contracts that tie managers to predetermined actions, these organizations use implicit performance contracts based on "relative improvement." While medium-term "stretch" goals are used as a framework for action plans, subsequent performance is evaluated and rewarded not on achieving the goal but on how well the team performed against world-class benchmarks, peers, competitors, and even prior periods.

Though there is still an implied contract to meet high performance standards, the key difference is that it is based on a set of relative measures. Such measures are self-regulating. They don't require an annual process of negotiation resulting in a fixed target. Such a contract does, however, imply more trust. Senior executives trust local managers to take whatever actions are necessary (within agreed parameters) to attain their goals. Local managers repay that trust by using their best endeavors to continuously strive for the maximum improvement. Making these changes enables the organization to respond faster to changing events and customer needs, and to reduce internal politics and game playing.

Chapter 3 tells the stories of three organizations that have gone beyond budgeting. Rhodia, a French global specialty chemicals company, abandoned budgeting in 1999. Borealis, a Danish petrochemicals company, abandoned budgeting in 1995. And Svenska Handelsbanken, a Swedish bank, abandoned budgeting in 1972. Chapter 4 looks at the principles and practices that can be derived from these (and other) cases and how they change behavior. Chapter 5 examines some of the lessons of implementation. It also looks at a number of U.S. and European companies that have had significant success using the principles of beyond budgeting but have subsequently been stymied by new owners or lack of support from the corporate center.

Part III deals with the second opportunity—how abandoning the budgeting process can enable radical decentralization. The concepts and principles of beyond budgeting present leaders with the opportunity they have been waiting for to finally break free from the command-and-control model. No matter how much they try to decentralize their operations, the fixed performance contract is a constant reminder of the command-and-control ethos.

The cutting of this umbilical cord enables front-line managers to take responsibility and use the full range of their capabilities to continuously improve their competitive position. Although they have more freedom and scope to perform, they are also more accountable for their performance. In other words, they can no longer hide in the nooks and crannies of the hierarchy, making excuses for poor performance. This model doesn't suit everyone. But those who take the challenge enjoy a stimulating and challenging work environment. It is a win-win situation for the organization and its employees.

This radical decentralization opportunity has the potential to create a special sort of competitive advantage based on releasing the energy and initiative of large numbers of capable and committed people. Chapter 6 looks at how three organizations have realized this opportunity. These include Ahlsell, a Swedish wholesaler; Leyland Trucks, a U.K. truck manufacturer; and Svenska Handelsbanken. We have used the Handelsbanken case again because it is the consummate beyond budgeting model.

Chapter 7 examines the roles that leaders must play in this transformation. Chapter 8 looks at how these leaders have changed centralized mind-sets. Again we draw on our case examples to provide valuable insights.

The fourth and final part of the book looks at how the adaptive and decentralized organization meets the vision of business leaders in the twenty-first-century organization. Chapter 9 examines how abandoning the budgeting process can release the full power of tools such as shareholder value models, the Balanced Scorecard, and rolling forecasts. These tools can each play a role in supporting the adaptive and decentralized organization. The new management culture unlocks the full potential of the tool, and the tool provides front-line people with the capabilities they need to succeed.

Finally, chapter 10 evaluates how the new model meets our three tests of success. We suggest it should provide a simple, low-cost, and more relevant alternative to budgeting. It should be in tune with the competitive environment. And it should promote good governance and more ethical behavior.

Most of the organizations we have examined have built a strong corporate culture based on each individual taking personal responsibility both for his or her own performance and for that of the team within which each works. Think of a golfer. Every golfer in the world worth his or her salt is inculcated from an early age in the moral standards expected on the golf course. Golfers keep their own score. There is transparency: Everyone knows each other's score. No one ever cheats on the course or misrepresents his or her score. To do so would bring disgrace and an abrupt end to the golfer's career. Nor do golfers need anyone telling them what score to aim for. They already know where they are in their own rankings list, whether it be at a local club or in a world competition. They know what they have to do to improve their handicap and advance sufficiently to raise their position relative to their peers. Their performance is continuously measured after each event. Their aim is continuous improvement.

These are moral and performance standards that many organizations aspire to but few have achieved. Those organizations that have succeeded in embedding the high moral standards of the golfing world into their corporate culture find they have little need for top-down budgets and fixed performance contracts. They set their people free to use their intuition and knowledge to make decisions close to the customer. This culture leads to a sustainable competitive advantage that is easier to describe than to analyze. It is also difficult to copy because it is based on trust.

The problem is that budgets and fixed performance contracts assume an absence of trust. They need to be replaced with a new contract based on the assumption that people will use their best endeavors to continuously improve performance. Trust is a step-by-step approach in building confidence. It has to be earned. No one is saying it is easy. It takes courage to challenge and ultimately change deeply ingrained management practices. But if faster response, lower costs, loyal customers, more ethical practices, and sustained competitive success are high on your agenda, then your courage will be richly rewarded.

Part I

The Promise of Beyond Budgeting

Chapter One

The Annual Performance Trap

> Uncertainty—in the economy, society, politics—has become so great as to render futile, if not counterproductive, the kind of planning most companies still practice: forecasting based on probabilities.[1]
> —PETER DRUCKER

Like them or loathe them, everyone has a view about budgets. CEOs like the warm feeling they get when they see the year-end profit forecasts. But they might be anxious about the reliability of the assumptions and the firm's ability to respond to change. CFOs like the way they are able to tie operating managers to fixed performance contracts (fixed targets reinforced by incentives). But they also know that the process takes too long and adds too little value. Operating managers like "knowing where they stand." But they are also concerned about the time wasted and, more important, that fixed performance contracts lead to decision paralysis and cosmetic accounting rather than decisive action and ethical reporting.

Though this ambivalence toward budgeting has existed for decades, the balance of opinion has swung decidedly in favor of the "very dissatisfied." Even within the financial management community, nine of ten have expressed their dissatisfaction, finding the budgeting process too "unreliable" and "cumbersome."[2] According to a recent cover article in

Fortune magazine, around 70 percent of companies surveyed were poor at executing strategy—a massive indictment of the performance management capabilities of budgets.[3] It turned out that most companies were characterized by incremental thinking, sclerotic budgeting processes, centralized decision making, petty operating rules, and controllers who demanded answers to the wrong questions. It is perhaps not so surprising that financial directors now rank budgetary reform as their top priority.[4] We will examine why these high levels of dissatisfaction have arisen in a moment. First, we must define what we mean by "budgeting."

One recent management accounting textbook defined a budget as a "quantitative expression of the money inflows and outflows to determine whether a financial plan will meet organizational goals."[5] But such a plan is the result of a protracted process. We have used a broader definition, one that defines budgeting not so much as a financial plan but as the *performance management process* that leads to and executes that plan. So when we use the word *budgeting* from here on, we mean the entire performance management process. This process is about agreeing upon and coordinating targets, rewards, action plans, and resources for the year ahead, and then measuring and controlling performance against that agreement. This process, the resultant negotiated fixed performance contracts, and their impact on management behavior are the focus of attention in this book.

How have we arrived at such high levels of dissatisfaction with budgeting? There are three primary factors: (1) Budgeting is cumbersome and too expensive, (2) budgeting is out of kilter with the competitive environment and no longer meets the needs of either executives or operating managers, and (3) the extent of "gaming the numbers" has risen to unacceptable levels. These problems have not happened overnight. Budgeting has been a festering sore for many decades, but its problems have, by and large, been swept under the carpet. It has taken the rapid changes in the competitive climate of the 1990s and the corporate governance scandals of 2001–2002 to expose them fully.

Budgeting Is Cumbersome and Too Expensive

For most participants, the budgeting process is an annual ritual that is deeply embedded in the corporate calendar. It absorbs huge amounts of time for an uncertain benefit. It typically begins at least four months prior to the year to which it relates. As figure 1-1 illustrates, it starts with a mission statement that sets out some of the aims of the business. This is followed by a group strategic plan that sets the direction and high-level goals of the firm. These form the framework for a budgeting process that grinds its way through countless meetings at which points are traded as targets are negotiated and resources agreed upon.

It starts when budget "packs" are sent out from the corporate center to operating divisions and departments, accompanied by forms to be completed that include sales, operational, and capital expenditure forecasts. For a whole business unit, the bottom line will be a profit and cash flow forecast for the year ahead. Once completed, these packs are returned to the corporate center (or to intermediary points in the hierarchy) and then subjected to review. Thereafter multiple iterations take place as each unit negotiates the final outcome. Once the budget is agreed upon, regular reports are required by the corporate center to enable senior executives to control performance.

FIGURE 1 - 1

The Traditional Budgeting Process

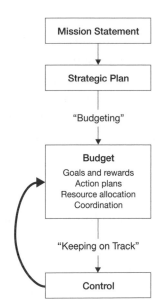

Despite the advent of powerful computer networks and multilayered models, this process remains protracted and expensive. The average time consumed is between four and five months.[6] It also involves many people and absorbs up to 20 to 30 percent of senior executives' and financial managers' time.[7] Some organizations have attempted to place a cost on the whole planning and budgeting process. Ford Motor Company figured out this amounted to $1.2 billion per annum.[8] A 1998 benchmarking study showed that the average company invested more than 25,000 person-days per billion dollars of revenue in the planning and performance measurement processes.[9]

The perception of the value provided by the budgeting process varies widely. In one firm we visited it was apparent that the group board thought the budget gave them control, whereas operating managers thought it was completely irrelevant to their needs. One of the primary reasons that financial directors rank budgetary reform as their highest priority is that their staffs spend too little of their time adding value. One conclusion from a 1999 global best practices study was that finance staff spent 79 percent of their time on "lower value-added activities" and only 21 percent of their time analyzing the numbers.[10] Nor does it help when hard-pressed managers have to wait eleven days into the following month before they can compare monthly management accounting results with the budget.[11]

For any firms involved in mergers, acquisitions, disposals, and other reorganizations, the budgeting workload can be overwhelming. The result is a finance team under constant pressure to reconfigure the numbers rather than support hard-pressed managers with the information they need to make decisions. A few comments in a recent survey of U.S. accountants are telling. "We have just been burning people out. They have been working incredible hours. . . . They are giving up family life. . . . We are all concerned."[12]

Budgeting Is Out of Kilter with the Competitive Environment and No Longer Meets the Needs of Either Executives or Operating Managers

If you had asked senior executives in the 1970s what they wanted from their management processes, they would likely have emphasized the need to set reasonable return-on-capital targets and then formulate detailed and coordinated plans for the year ahead to meet them. Executives would have expected compliance with these plans throughout the organization, supported by tight cost control and measures geared to monitoring performance against the plan. In other words, they expected to plan, coordinate, and control their operations from the corporate center.

The budgeting process was tailor-made for the job (although it was already becoming cumbersome and expensive). IBM was a classic example. In 1973 its planning bureaucracy had grown to three thousand people and its "annual" planning process approached an eighteen-month cycle.[13] But it played a part in enabling the company to become the dominant player in the global computer market. Its ability to design, make, and sell its computer hardware and software to compliant customers was supreme. Every division, business unit, and individual salesperson knew from their performance contracts what they had to achieve in the year ahead. Growth and prosperity seemed unstoppable.

The oil price increases and subsequent inflationary pressures of the mid-1970s changed the competitive climate. Leaders became concerned about rising costs. Bloated bureaucracies and their associated fixed costs were a key factor, and a number of managers began to realize that the budgeting process failed to challenge them. One solution promoted by consultants was called *zero-base budgeting* (ZBB). ZBB starts with a blank sheet of paper in regard to discretionary expenditure. It proved to be a useful (though usually one-off) exercise to review discretionary overheads. However, the process was so bureaucratic and time-consuming that few companies used it more than once. Moreover, like traditional budgeting, it was based on the organizational hierarchy. It thus reinforced functional barriers and failed to focus on the opportunities for improving business processes.

In the late 1980s, IBM stumbled badly as it misread the personal computer revolution and found itself surrounded by more nimble competitors with lower costs. Like many other firms, it had to make tough decisions as it faced gut-wrenching changes, or it would fail to survive. Discontinuous change had become the norm (see figure 1-2).

From the 1980s onward, uncertainty increased and the pressures on corporate performance became more intense. Shareholders were demanding that firms be at or near the top of their industry peer group

FIGURE 1 - 2

The Changing Business Environment

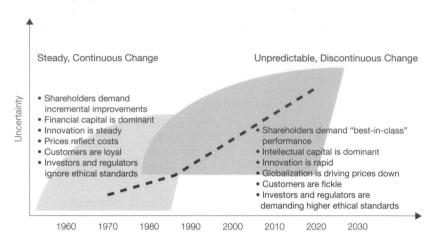

on a range of measures. Intellectual capital such as brands, loyal customers, and proven management teams had risen to be the primary drivers of shareholder value. Product and strategy cycles had shortened, emphasizing the need to continuously innovate. Prices and margins were constantly under pressure, requiring action to slash structural costs and reduce bureaucracy. And customers were increasingly fickle, calling out for more decentralized authority to enable front-line people to respond to changing customer needs. Moreover, "command and control" had become a pejorative term for an outdated management style. Leaders had recognized that to become more "agile" or "adaptive" meant transferring more power and authority to people closer to the customer.

In these turbulent times the budgeting process struggled to cope. Goals and measures were internally focused. Intellectual capital was outside the orbit of the budgetary control system. Innovation was stifled by rigid adherence to fixed plans and resource allocations agreed to twelve to eighteen months earlier. Costs were fiercely protected by departmental managers who saw them as budget entitlements rather than scarce resources. The internal focus on maximizing volume collided with the external focus on satisfying customers' needs. And far from being empowered to respond to strategic change, front-line people found that it was easier to do nothing than to try to get multiple signatures on a document authorizing a change in the plan.

Many firms responded to changes in the competitive climate by introducing more frequent and streamlined planning and budgeting processes. These included budgets done half-yearly or quarterly instead of annually, and "rolling budgets" that tended to have a twelve-month horizon (updated every quarter). Though these approaches offered more current (and thus more relevant) numbers for managers to follow, they suffered from an increased workload (even if done with fewer line items) and thus, more often than not, even higher cost.

Implementing strategic management models such as the Balanced Scorecard was another approach taken by an increasing number of firms that tried to shift their emphasis from being "budget-focused" to being "strategy-focused" organizations. The Balanced Scorecard is one of the most innovative tools to emerge in recent years and offers organizations a robust framework for overcoming many of the problems we have just outlined. But its full power is too often constrained by the short-term performance drivers of the annual budget. These remain focused on "managing" the next year-end rather than supporting medium-term strategy. Indeed, the evidence from Scorecard users is that, far from transforming their companies into strategy-focused organizations, they have simply added some strategic indicators to their annual budgets. Scorecard indicators, according to a 2002 global survey, remained predominantly financial (62 percent) and lagging (76 percent).[14] Moreover, in many cases, Scorecard targets are compared with actuals, and variances are reported in a similar way to the traditional budget.

Few of the innovative management tools of the past decade have been used to fundamentally transform the performance management process. At best they have made marginal improvements to a broken system. At worst they have had negative effects as they ruptured the coherence of a flawed but otherwise working traditional model. Few have achieved their potential.

The Extent of "Gaming the Numbers" Has Risen to Unacceptable Levels

Budgets started life in the 1920s as tools for managing costs and cash flows in such large industrial organizations as DuPont, General Motors, ICI, and Siemens. It wasn't until the 1960s that they mutated into fixed performance contracts. It was at this time, according to Professor Tom

Johnson, coauthor of the ground-breaking book *Relevance Lost: The Rise and Fall of Management Accounting* (and one of the United States' foremost accounting historians), that companies "increasingly used accounting results such as costs, net income, or return-on-investment (ROI) not just to keep score, but also to motivate the actions of operating personnel at all levels."[15]

By the early 1970s a new generation of leaders, schooled in the finer arts of financial planning, began to use financial indicators to manage the business. As Johnson points out,

> [A]ccounting results dominated most managers' attention to the point where they no longer knew, or cared, about the production, technological, and marketing determinants of competitiveness. By 1970, moreover, business education itself reinforced the practice of managing through the accounting numbers.[16]

This led to the increased use of fixed performance contracts as the basis of setting fixed targets against which performance was evaluated and rewarded. The fixed performance contract typically begins with an "earnings" contract between senior executives and external parties (such as investors or bankers) and then cascades down the organization in the form of "budget" contracts between senior executives and operating managers.

The budget contract is usually fixed for a period of twelve months. Its purpose is to *commit* a subordinate or team to achieving an agreed-upon outcome and then to enable a superior to *control* the results against that outcome (reserving the right to interfere and change the terms if necessary). The terms of such a contract typically include the following:

- *A fixed target.* Targets are fixed for the year ahead and specified in terms of financial numbers. Typical targets include sales, profits, costs, and ratios such as return on capital.
- *An incentive or reward.* Incentives are usually fixed to the agreed target and cover a range of outcomes (e.g., from just below the target to just above the target). Other positive outcomes, such as recognition or promotion, can also be contingent on the achievement of targets.
- *An agreed-upon plan.* A plan expressed in strategic and financial terms will usually be attached to the contract. The process lead-

ing to this agreement can be top down, prepared by leaders or central planning departments, or more likely bottom up, with local teams preparing their plans and then negotiating and agreeing upon them with superiors.

- *A statement of resources.* Once plans have been agreed upon, the "master budget" can be prepared and resources allocated to functions and departments. Each contract will have a budget statement encompassing the resources (both capital and operational) attached to the plan.
- *A commitment to cross-company actions.* The agreement will specify the commitments that one business or operating unit makes to another. For example, production units must commit to meeting the sales plan.
- *A reporting schedule.* The agreement will specify the type and frequency of reporting. Senior executives will normally have the right to step in and demand corrective action to ensure that performance remains on track with the agreed plan. Managers will also need to explain any variances and provide updated forecasts as a basis of such action.

The terms and conditions of this contract can either be explicit (usually a written letter from a superior to a subordinate) or implicit (custom and practice tell the parties what the likely outcomes will be). It is not, of course, legally binding. It is more of a promise or a commitment than a legal transaction. And its interpretation can be different across and within organizations. Indeed, budget contracts range from highly authoritative to highly participative.

If used in a responsible way, such contracts provide the basis for a clear understanding between organizational levels and enable senior executives to maintain control over multiple divisions and business units. The problem, however, is that in the wrong hands, such a contract leads to undesirable and dysfunctional outcomes at every level of the organization. These problems multiply as the pressure to improve performance rises, especially if, at the same time, economic conditions are deteriorating.

Few senior executives seem to be aware of these problems. They see outcomes in terms of numbers rather than behaviors. In this context, budget contracts can act like drugs. They seduce executives into believing that they have control over their future financial outcomes. But, like most drugs, they have serious side effects. They lead both senior executives and operating managers into an annual performance trap from which it is difficult to escape. All actions focus on the current fiscal year. It is when the gap between key budget assumptions and emerging reality widens to the point at which the two bear little relation to each other that the problems begin. Few CEOs want to miss their earnings targets and risk ridicule in the media and the investor community. Equally few operating managers want to see adverse variances, risking the wrath of their superiors as well as missing bonuses and promotions.

The all too frequent outcome is that organizations resort to such practices as "managing their earnings" (e. g., at Gillette, Coca-Cola, and Citicorp).[17] In some cases it leads to outright fraud (e.g., at Enron and WorldCom). The fear of failure, more often than not, is the underlying cause. This was evident at both Enron and WorldCom. The WorldCom culture, say those who worked there, was all about living up to CEO Bernard Ebbers's demands. "You would have a budget, and he would mandate that you had to be 2 percent under budget. Nothing else was acceptable."[18]

These are not isolated cases. Business magazines and newspapers have been replete with similar examples of malpractice. They result from senior executives and operating managers committing to overly aggressive targets and then fudging the numbers to meet them. None of this is new. A number of British accounting scandals in the late 1980s and early 1990s, including Maxwell Communications, Pollypeck, and Colorol, should have alerted investors and executives to the dangers of the fixed performance contract. Though corporate governance procedures were tightened in their aftermath, the underlying lessons were ignored.

These high profile cases have captured the attention of the investment community. But such practices are also rife deep inside many other organizations. One major study of over four hundred U.S. companies in 1987 found that budget games and manipulation were widespread, noting that:

> Deferring a needed expenditure [was the budget game] used with
> the greatest frequency. . . . Getting approvals after money was spent,
> shifting funds between accounts to avoid budget overruns, and
> employment of contract labor to avoid exceeding headcount limits

are the other relatively popular games. Almost all respondents state that they engage in one or more of the budget games.[19]

Many front-line managers need to use their political skills more than ever to keep them out of trouble. This applies not only to the planning and budgeting process (one recent survey showed that 66 percent of respondents believed that their planning process was influenced more by politics than by strategy[20]), but also to the process of setting targets and evaluating performance. Many examples of dysfunctional behavior driven by fixed performance contracts have been given to us in the course of our research. Here are ten typical comments:

1. *"Always negotiate the lowest targets and the highest rewards."* This is the desired outcome of the budgeting process from the manager's perspective—a target that is inwardly comfortable to you, yet appears outwardly difficult to your superior.

2. *"Always make the bonus, whatever it takes."* Any actions that need to be taken to reach the maximum bonus are fair game. Stuffing the distribution channel with "sale-or-return" products is a classic example.

3. *"Never put customer care above sales targets."* Though everyone wants to satisfy customers, that is not how they are measured and rewarded. So they meet the sales target, persuade customers to buy their products, and convince them that their slow-moving stock really is a great deal!

4. *"Never share knowledge or resources with other teams—they are the enemy!"* The main competition is not in the external marketplace. It is with other divisions, business units, and departments, all trying to obtain a higher share of the central resource pool than you. There is also the NIH ("not invented here") syndrome to block any sharing initiatives. The arrogance and inflated egos of business leaders prevent good ideas being taken on board.

5. *"Always ask for more resources than you need, expecting to be cut back to what you actually need."* This merely anticipates the negotiation process. Superiors will always want to reduce your requirements, so by increasing your demands, you are more likely to end up with what you want.

6. *"Always spend what's in the budget."* "Use it or lose it" is the manager's mantra. Not spending the budget is a cardinal sin in most organizations. The result is that superiors invariably question why the resource is needed and are understandably reluctant to allow it to pass into the budget for the next period.

7. *"Always have the ability to explain adverse variances."* One of the first skills a junior manager learns in any organization is how to explain away an adverse variance. There will always be some cause beyond your control. But you know that financial variances reveal little about the real causes of problems. Often these can be "upstream" in another department. For example, although salespeople have to deal with customer complaints, these are often caused by poor order taking, wrong deliveries, or inadequate training.

8. *"Never provide accurate forecasts."* Never share bad news while you still have time to do something about it. Superiors will either berate you for your poor performance or demand a higher than agreed result because of some unexpected additional revenue that was not generated by your efforts. The other approach is to tell your superior what he or she wants to hear and trust in your good fortune.

9. *"Always meet the numbers, never beat them."* Managing the results (also known as cooking the books) is a frequent outcome of budgeting. Many finance managers are well versed in "managing the slack" and feeding it into the results when needed. However, as we have seen, this practice can border on outright fraud.

10. *"Never take risks."* It is just not worth it. If it's not in the budget, you might be exposed. Anyhow, if you did take a risk and it worked out well, your superior probably thought of it first! And if it didn't work out, your job might be on the line.

Of course, not all the blame can be placed on the shoulders of the budgeting process. As noted earlier, like all management processes, it is *how it is used* that is important. However, the increasing propensity to use it as the springboard for aggressive performance contracts between companies and investors and between parents and subsidiaries has turned the budget into an annual performance trap. By 2001, the fixed performance contract had become accepted practice in the majority of global corporations. According to a 2002 survey of two thousand global companies, the linkage between fixed targets and incentives was confirmed in 60 percent of cases.[21]

The fixed performance contract is a deadly virus at the core of many organizations today. It can lie dormant for years until an aggressive "management by the numbers" leader comes along and activates its viral properties. It is a dismal way of managing a business.

Toward a Vision of a New Management Model

Although very few firms have attempted to reengineer their whole management model, most leaders would likely agree that the model should support the organization's main goals. What are these goals? While each leader will have his or her own list, we have selected six generic goals: to satisfy shareholders by achieving sustained competitive success, to find and keep the best people, to be innovative, to operate with low costs, to satisfy customers profitably, and to maintain effective governance and promote ethical reporting.

If these goals are representative of how leaders see their organizations in the future, they are a long way from where most of them are now. The traditional budgeting model conflicts with every one of those goals. We need a new management model that eliminates these conflicts and positively supports these goals.

Leaders need to act. This is indeed what a number of them have done. The rest of this book is about their experiences. We will show how they have adopted a coherent set of management processes that are less complex, less expensive, and more relevant than those they have replaced. Some have achieved their visions. Others are making progress. And some have slipped backward as new leaders have undone much good work. By liberating their people from the fixed performance contract, most are transforming themselves into organizations fit to compete in a twenty-first-century environment in which the only certainty is uncertainty and change.

Chapter Summary

- The budget, or to be more precise, the budgeting process, is universally disliked. It takes too long, costs too much, and adds too little value.
- The budgeting model is also out of kilter with a competitive environment that is now subject to discontinuous change. Shareholders now demand that firms be at or near the top of their industry peer group on a range of measures. Intellectual capital, including brands and loyal customers, has risen to be the primary driver of shareholder value. Product and strategy cycles have shortened. Prices and margins are constantly under pressure, requiring action to slash structural costs and reduce bureaucracy. And customers are increasingly fickle, calling out for more decentralized authority to enable front-line people to respond to changing customer needs. All of these changes make it more difficult for managers to operate with budgets that were designed for a more stable environment.
- Whereas the *budget* is a simple estimate of future income and expenditure and has few behavioral implications, the *budgeting process* typically results in a fixed performance contract between superiors and subordinates and is one of the primary drivers of managerial behavior. Budgets and fixed performance contracts are now being used to drive and evaluate managerial performance. This can (and often does) cause managers to behave in dysfunctional ways at every stage in the budgeting process, particularly if they find they cannot meet these contracts. At best this results in "managing the numbers." At worst it results in outright misrepresentation and fraud.
- Though some progress has been made to make budgeting faster, cheaper, and more strategic, few firms have been able to overcome the undesirable (and often pervasive) behavioral side effects caused by the fixed performance contract.
- We need an alternative management model that supports the goals of businesses in the twenty-first century. But achieving this

vision requires more than fixing broken budgets. It requires a new set of management processes, and a new style of leadership. Moreover, it requires a new *coherence* among these management processes and leadership principles to liberate the full potential of the organization and its people.

Chapter Two

Breaking Free

Many organizations talk about decentralization but few know how
to do it right. . . . Decentralization is 10 percent what you say and
90 percent what you do.
—ARNE MÅRTENSSON, CHAIRMAN, SVENSKA HANDELSBANKEN

We have spent the past five years visiting many organizations that have,
to some degree or other, attempted to tackle the problems of budgeting.
Most have gone beyond tinkering with the existing process: They have
abandoned it altogether. They have eliminated the annual cycle of
preparing, submitting, negotiating, and finally agreeing upon a budget
by department, function, business unit, division, and finally the whole
organization. The result has been to save months of work. The budget
no longer represents an annual fixed performance contract that defines
what subordinates must deliver to superiors for the year ahead. The
budget no longer determines how resources are allocated. The budget no
longer determines what business units must make and sell. And the
budget no longer determines how the performance of those units and
their people will be evaluated and rewarded.

Who are these organizations? They don't conform to any industry
pattern. They include two banks, a petrochemicals company, a distributor, a car manufacturer, a charity, a brewer, a furniture retailer, a truck

manufacturer, an eye care company, a computer manufacturer, a tele-communications company, a ball-bearings manufacturer, a food producer, and a specialty chemicals company. They are headquartered in Sweden, the United Kingdom, France, Norway, Denmark, Holland, and the United States. They vary in size from a small charity to a huge, complex, global organization with thousands of products.

What have they done differently? It varies. Some have seen budgeting as an ineffective process that is too long and costly and that fails to provide its users with sufficient value. They have seen the opportunity to build more responsive and value-adding processes, to make them less political and to have fewer behavioral side effects. Others have seen the problem more in terms of how budgets reinforce bureaucracy and are barriers to cultural change (especially how they block empowerment initiatives). They have seen the opportunity to release the pent-up energy and imagination of thousands of front-line people and to open the way to (permanently) lower costs and more sustainable profitability. But the one common thread is that these organizations do not manage with an annual budget. And they have used the same principles to replace it.

This chapter describes how companies have gone beyond budgeting and seized noteworthy opportunities, especially enabling more adaptive management processes and enabling a more radically decentralized organization.

The Adaptive Process Opportunity:
Enabling Managers to Focus on Continuous Value Creation

Rhodia is a large specialty chemical company with sales of $7.2 billion operating in many global consumer markets. The annual budgeting process exceeded six months to complete. It was slowing down response, so in 1999 the company replaced it with two performance management cycles. One takes a strategic view and continually looks two to five years ahead, with an annual review. The other takes an operational view and looks five to eight quarters ahead, with a quarterly review. Managers now focus on medium-term strategy rather than short-term fixed targets, and on taking actions to support key value drivers rather than negotiating and then following fixed plans and detailed numbers. Senior executives believe that these rolling reviews (supported by rolling forecasts) give them more control than the budget ever did. Moreover, managers now have the capability to respond more effectively to emerging threats and opportunities.

The approach taken by Rhodia is typical of many organizations we have reported upon. The following subsections briefly describe what these organizations used to do with their budgeting processes, what they now do without them, and what they have gained. These issues are covered in much more detail in chapters 3, 4, and 5.

Setting Targets

WHAT THEY USED TO DO. The organizations we have researched used to set targets on the basis of financial numbers that, more often than not, were negotiated between superiors and subordinates before the start of the year. These numbers were fixed for the year ahead and represented the key component of the annual fixed performance contract. All actions were then focused on meeting the numbers. However, whether this process maximized the profit potential of the firm is doubtful given the desire for superiors to "stretch ambition" and the desire for budget holders to play safe. Jack Welch, for one, believes that "making a budget is an exercise in minimalization. You're always trying to get the lowest out of people, because everyone is negotiating to get the lowest number."[1] The main losers are the shareholders, because neither short-term profits nor longer-term wealth creation reaches its potential.

WHAT THEY DO NOW. They now set targets based on high-level key performance indicators (KPIs) such as return-on-capital, free cash flows, or cost-to-income ratios. Goals are typically set at levels aimed at maximizing short- and medium-term profit potential at every level of the business. Managers are willing to accept (or propose) these stretch goals because their performance will not be evaluated and rewarded against them. They will subsequently be measured and rewarded using a range of relative indicators such as peer group performance, internal and external benchmarks, and prior years' results. "Baseline" goals set a lower reference level of expectations. Though goals are primarily financial at the highest level, they become more operational the nearer they are to the front line.

WHAT THEY HAVE GAINED. The benefits are that the process of setting targets is fast (days rather than months) and because it is based on relative measures it will seldom need to be reset. Also, because the benchmarking bar is always being raised, it is more likely to maximize profit potential. Some project leaders figure they have saved 95 percent of the time that used to be spent on budgeting and forecasting. This time is more usefully spent on planning how to create more value for customers and shareholders as well as how to respond more effectively to change.

Rewarding People

WHAT THEY USED TO DO. They assumed that managers would be motivated and fairly rewarded if the right mix of targets and incentives was put in place. Thus, rewards were linked to a fixed outcome agreed to in advance. The benefits were that managers knew where they stood and what they had to meet. It was then up to them to achieve the target and bonus. Leaders knew (and therefore accepted) that this element of the budget contract led to gaming.

WHAT THEY DO NOW. At most firms, performance is evaluated and rewarded based on a formula related to how teams compare with benchmarks, peers, and prior years. One firm uses a formula for a business unit that includes growth versus previous year, growth versus the competition, profit versus the previous year, profit versus the competition, debt versus the previous year, and quality versus the previous year. Another firm has dispensed with local rewards altogether and for the past thirty years has been using one groupwide profit-sharing scheme based on a formula related to the competitive performance of the firm. Though these approaches vary, the common factors are that rewards are divorced from *fixed* annual targets negotiated *in advance*. Rewards are also based on the performance of teams rather than individuals.

WHAT THEY HAVE GAINED. One benefit is that all cases have seen a reduction in gaming behavior (with no fixed contract, there is little point in gaming). Moreover, these organizations also believe that they recognize and reward the best performers, not just those who are skilled at negotiating budgets or those who have been fortunate to hit a market on the upturn that wasn't anticipated at the time of the budget agreement. They also find that their approaches reward longer-term value creation and recognize that this is delivered by interdependent teams rather than individuals.

Action Planning

WHAT THEY USED TO DO. The planning process used to be an annual cycle, driven by top management. This process was either top down, prepared by leaders or central planning departments, or bottom up, with local teams preparing their plans and then negotiating and agreeing on them with superiors. Many were based on departmental improvements that were not necessarily in accord with broader strategic objectives. After many months of discussion, the resulting plan provided clear guidelines that told people what they had to do in the year ahead. However, such a predetermined plan can be a liability when the business environment has become as unpredictable as it is today.

The evidence suggests that such problems with the traditional model are typically ignored. For example, only 20 percent of firms change their budgets within the fiscal cycle.[2] Another jolting survey result shows that 85 percent of management teams spend less than one hour per month discussing strategy.[3]

WHAT THEY DO NOW. Responsibility for strategy reviews is devolved to business units and, in some cases, front-line teams. They are responsible not for meeting agreed-upon budgets, but for taking actions that maximize value for customers and shareholders. The role of group executives is to set high-level strategic objectives and medium-term goals, and then to challenge the plans and initiatives that managers propose to ensure that they represent the best options available and that their core assumptions and risks are reasonable. Business unit teams review the medium-term outlook (goals, strategies, value drivers, and action plans) every year and the short-term outlook (actual and forecast performance indicators and operating decisions) every quarter. Both cycles are aimed at achieving the same aspirational goals. In some cases, these cycles have merged into one continuous review process at the level of the operating team. Useful tools such as rolling forecasts, the Balanced Scorecard, and activity accounting support these performance reviews. Action plans are derived from them.

WHAT THEY HAVE GAINED. Making strategy an open, continuous, and adaptive process enables front-line teams to focus on value creation, to anticipate threats and opportunities, and to respond to the changing needs of customers. They are also able to align their goals, rewards, actions, and measures with strategy as it evolves. This alignment means that management actions are consistent with strategic goals rather than with narrowly based departmental interests.

Managing Resources

WHAT THEY USED TO DO. The organizations we studied used to allocate resources on the basis of budget contracts negotiated *in advance* together with a share of "central costs" that (in theory, if not in practice) were needed to support them. The benefit was that at one point in time all resources were allocated to one unit or another. No further management attention was then needed until the following year's budget review. However, senior executives too often acted like central committees, approving or disapproving investment proposals based on annual plans. It is little wonder that strategy expert Gary Hamel described this approach as "the last bastion of Soviet-style central planning."[4]

WHAT THEY DO NOW. They make resources available and accessible to front-line teams as and when required through fast-track approvals and easier access to operational resources. Some have created a high-level team that manages the resource portfolio (with quarterly reviews). This approach overcomes much of the game playing associated with resource allocation. They manage operational resources by setting goals based on KPIs (e.g., a cost-to-income ratio) within which managers can operate. In one firm, the goal was to reduce fixed costs by 30 percent over five years. Managers are held accountable *after the event* for the deployment of these resources in the value creation process. Some firms have developed an "internal market" whereby resources can be acquired by operating units from central service providers at an agreed-upon price.

WHAT THEY HAVE GAINED. Devolving more resource decisions to front-line teams has the effect not only of making the organization more responsive, but also of making managers more accountable for resource decisions. This, in turn, builds greater ownership and leads to less waste. Moreover, with no budget to act as a floor for costs, the way is clear for managers to seek permanent reductions in their continuous quest for higher levels of efficiency and profitability.

Coordinating Actions

WHAT THEY USED TO DO. They linked their plans through the central coordination of annual departmental and business unit budgets. For example, they ensured that production and sales were in tune, and that marketing had the resources to support the sales plan. At that point in time each unit plan linked with another, leading to a coherent plan for the whole firm. But although the plans of individual departments might have been coordinated with each other, it was doubtful whether this amounted to a coherent *strategy* for the firm as a whole (one study concluded that 60 percent of firms fail to align their action plans with their strategy).[5] Departmental managers are often too keen to improve their own department without considering how this may fit with broader strategic goals. Moreover, in a rapidly changing environment, it is not enough to coordinate plans just once a year. A more dynamic process is needed.

WHAT THEY DO NOW. They coordinate their plans and actions across the business not through a central plan, but through service-level agreements that cover a period appropriate to the customer order cycle. This can vary from dealing with individual customized requests to anticipating and managing the periodic demand of customer segments. Inside the firm, these arrangements take the form of service-level agreements that, in effect, are commitments from one process to another based on anticipated demand.

WHAT THEY HAVE GAINED. Where feasible, operating capacity rises and falls according to prevailing demand. There is less waste as fewer items are "made for stock." With such an approach, the organization acts like an integrated system pursuing a common strategy rather than a collection of disparate parts. It also encourages sharing and cooperation and focuses on providing the external (paying) customer with a seamless solution and excellent service.

Measuring and Controlling Performance

WHAT THEY USED TO DO. All of the organizations we studied used to control performance against predetermined budgets and then took corrective action to ensure that performance remained on track. Thus, local managers would need to explain any variances and provide updated budgets or forecasts as a basis for further action. They would rarely look beyond the next fiscal year-end. (In 77 percent of the 2,000 global companies surveyed by the Hackett Group in 2002, the focus of the forecast process was on the remaining period of the current fiscal year.[6])

WHAT THEY DO NOW. Executives and operating managers at all levels see the same information at the same time. Moreover, they focus more on trends and forecasts than on the "rear-view mirror." Main features include leading indicators, rolling forecasts, KPI comparisons with external benchmarks, and performance-league tables. These are combined with actual financial results, comparisons against prior years, and trend analysis to provide a rich (and constantly moving) performance picture.

WHAT THEY HAVE GAINED. There is less dependence on a one-dimensional control system. A much richer, open, and transparent control system is used to inform managers at all levels about performance at all levels. With no fixed target to meet, there is no need for middle managers to manipulate the figures or present them in such a misleading way as to distort the real picture.

Relative Improvement Contracts

The overall effect of these changes is a performance management process based on a *relative improvement contract* rather than on fixed targets. It assumes that it is not wise to make managers commit to a fixed target and then control their future actions against it. The implicit agreement is that executives will provide a challenging and open operating environment and that employees will deliver continuous performance improvement using their knowledge and judgment to adapt to changing conditions. It is based on mutual trust, but it is not a soft alternative to the fixed performance contract. High visibility of individual and team performance offers no hiding place. Managers must perform to high levels of expectation (relative to peers) or face the consequences. Table 2-1 shows how the fixed performance and relative improvement contracts support fundamentally different relationships between one organization level and another.

TABLE 2 - 1

Contrasting the Fixed Performance and Relative Improvement Contracts

	Fixed Performance Contract	Relative Improvement Contract
Targets	Your [sales/profit] target is fixed at [$x million].	We trust you to maximize your profit potential to continuously improve against the agreed-upon bench-marked KPIs and to remain in the top [quartile] of your peer group.
Rewards	Your rewards for reaching this target are [x%] of [profits], starting at 80% and capped at 120% of target.	You trust us to assess your rewards by a peer review panel based on your performance "with hindsight" at the end of each year.
Plans	Your agreed-upon action plans are attached to this contract.	We trust you to take whatever action is required to meet your medium-term goals within agreed-upon governance principles and strategic boundaries.
Resources	The agreed resources to support the capital and operating budgets are set out in the attached budget statements.	You trust us to provide the resources you need when you need them. We trust you to keep within agreed KPI boundaries.
Coordination	Your activities will be coordinated with other budget holders according to the agreed plan or as redirected by your superior.	We trust you to coordinate your activities with other teams according to periodic agreements and customer requirements.
Controls	Your performance will be monitored monthly. Any variations will be reviewed, and executives reserve the right to take further action. Forecasts in the form of [revised budgets] will be required on a [quarterly] basis.	We trust you to provide forecasts based on the most likely outcome. You trust us to monitor performance and interfere only when indicators/trends move out of bounds.

The difference is that, as table 2-1 shows, the performance emphasis has shifted from short-term fixed contracts with top-down control to medium-term relative contracts with multilevel control. This represents a gradual shift of performance responsibility from the center to lower levels in the organization. This is more than a change in the process of agreeing upon a contract—it is a cultural sea change. The core philosophies are different. The fixed performance contract is based on central control. It assumes the absence of trust. The relative improvement contract is based on self-regulation. It assumes that teams can be trusted to manage their own affairs (within agreed boundaries) and to be fully accountable for their results. This is a huge challenge for most leaders. They need to acknowledge that they cannot release the power of their "greatest assets" (their people) and continue to plan and control their detailed actions. They have to release the coils of the budgeting process and the fixed performance contract.

The impact on the behavior of front-line people must not be underestimated. It leads to what Harvard professor Chris Argyris calls "internal commitment." The hidden problem, according to Argyris, is that people have to deal with two types of commitment. First, there is *external commitment,* which, by and large, leads people to fulfill contractual obligations specified by others, and in which performance goals are top down. Second, there is *internal commitment,* which allows individuals to define their own plans and the tasks required to fulfill them, and which is participatory, comes from within the individual, and leads to people taking risks and accepting responsibility for their actions.[7] This is the behavior that the relative improvement contract seeks to encourage. The rhetoric of leaders does not produce internal commitment any more than it leads to effective empowerment or personal responsibility. Such changes require a fundamental change in the process that determines the behavioral context.

Coherence is the key. There must be coherence within the set of management processes used, and they must be a matching set, not a mix of the old and new. The budgeting model, for all its flaws, is coherent. All its principles and practices assume central control. Therefore, introducing foreign bodies such as relative improvement contracts that assume self-regulation will be rejected. It ruptures the coherence. The same applies to strategic models that assume that front-line managers have the capability to use them. Nor will rolling forecasts live up to expectations. Front-line people are hardly likely to tell central controllers about bad news if it means taking a verbal beating or having their targets reset. They are more likely to try to solve the problem on their own. Service-level agreements are another example. They assume that operating units are treated like real customers that can demand low charges and acceptable conditions of satisfaction. But if central service departments continue to hold the power centrally, then this relationship is doomed to failure.

The principles of *beyond budgeting* offer a new coherent management model. It assumes that front-line managers are able to regulate their own performance. Senior executives provide a supportive role. They challenge and coach, but decisions are taken locally within a clear governance framework based on principles, values, and boundaries. In this new coherence, relative improvement contracts, strategic models, rolling forecasts, and service-level agreements make sense. They all support the needs of front-line managers and provide senior executives with supervisory controls.

There must also be a wider coherence among the organization's success factors, its strategy, its management processes, its leadership style, and its culture. For most organizations today, their success factors have changed and their strategy is changing, but their management processes, leadership styles, and cultures are lagging behind. But for some organizations, fixing processes is only part of the solution. The real opportunity lies in the further possibilities that adopting management processes based on relative improvement contracts can open up. This process, as we shall see, is about lifting the burden of bureaucracy from the shoulders of front-line people, eradicating the dependency culture, and enabling people to accept even more responsibility for their own performance.

The Radical Decentralization Opportunity: Enabling Leaders to Create a High Performance Organization

Swedish bank Svenska Handelsbanken was struggling and losing customers, especially to a smaller rival run by Dr. Jan Wallander. So the bank invited him to join it as its new CEO. He accepted, but with certain demands, one of which was to radically decentralize operations and (to achieve this effectively) to abandon the budgeting process. Since Wallander's stewardship began, the bank has outperformed its Nordic rivals on just about every measure you can think of, including return on equity, total shareholder return, earnings per share, cost-to-income ratio, and customer satisfaction.

Convincing others that the organization should not be coordinated and controlled from the center was a tough challenge. Wallander was resolute, however. He believed that what holds the organization together is not a plan, but a commitment to a clear purpose and to a set of clearly articulated principles and values. It is these that provide the coherence for coordinated actions. He is fond of saying that the only "organization chart" at the bank is the internal telephone directory. If everyone knows his or her part in the value delivery system and plays it well, then the result will be satisfied and profitable customers. Customers can sense the power of such a system. They know if processes are working in harmony and if front-line people have the power to deal with their requirements. They can feel the experience. And because it is so rare, they will return again and again.

Above all, Wallander believed in setting people free. Free from stifling bureaucracies, free from the restrictions of predetermined plans, free from the fear of failing to meet fixed targets, and free from the forced cross-company actions designed by central planners. But he also knew that this freedom depended on opening up the information system. To restrict its flow or to attempt to control it made no sense. He insisted on only one set of numbers, or "one truth," with no internal profit taking. Only by enabling everyone to see the same information at the same time would the right questions be asked and the right decisions taken. Sharing and cooperation were no longer choices. They happened automatically.

Why Is Radical Decentralization Desirable?

The delegation of decision-making and spending authority has always been one of the key functions of budgeting. However, this delegation usually occurs strictly within a regime of compliance and control. It differs significantly from the approach taken by organizations such as Handelsbanken, which have gone much further and transferred power from the center to operating managers and their teams, vesting in them the authority to use their judgment and initiative to achieve results *without being constrained by some specific plan or agreement*. Thus, devolution of responsibility is about enabling and encouraging local decisions, not dictating and directing them.

The merits of empowerment have been recognized for decades. Indeed they have been the subject of academic research and discussion for well over fifty years. Writers such as Mayo, McGregor, Maslow, Herzberg, and Drucker have all argued in one form or another that superior performance is driven not by planning, controls, and incentives, but by team working, self-esteem, and personal development. And more recently, such writers as Senge, Wheatley, Johnson, Mintzberg, Schein, Pfeffer, and Argyris have all argued against "managing by numbers" and for greater team-based responsibility and self-regulation.

Research has also shown that employees are at their most satisfied when they are able to participate in decisions.[8] Young, talented people are well aware of these issues. A 1997 McKinsey survey of 6,900 U.S. managers concluded that the top three reasons why they chose one firm over another were "values and culture" (58 percent), "freedom and autonomy" (56 percent), and "exciting challenge" (51 percent).[9] Though this survey was conducted in the midst of the dot-com boom, it remains the case that talented managers can obtain the same compensation package at all major companies—the difference lies in the opportunities for challenge, personal development, and growth. Thus, it is hardly surprising that they gravitate to those firms that have flat, devolved, team-based structures.

Handelsbanken abandoned budgeting to devolve performance responsibility to front-line people. That was Wallander's vision. Though not connected to Wallander, other leaders have followed a similar path. These include Jean-Marie Descarpentries, first at Carnaud Metal Box and later at the French computer company Groupe Bull. John Oliver and Charlie Poskett, after trying every conceivable improvement initiative at U.K. truck maker Leyland Trucks, discovered that empowering front-line teams was the approach needed to transform performance. And Gunnar Haglund at Swedish distributor Ahlsell turned the company around by radically decentralizing performance responsibility in the late 1990s.

These leaders have shared six common principles. They have:

1. Built a governance framework based on clear principles and boundaries
2. Created a high-performance climate based on the visibility of relative success at every level
3. Provided front-line teams with the freedom to make decisions that are consistent with governance principles and strategic goals
4. Placed the responsibility for value creating decisions on teams
5. Focused teams on customer outcomes
6. Supported open and ethical information systems

Building a Clear Governance Framework

WHAT THEY HAVE ABANDONED. The leaders in question have abandoned the notion that employees base their commitment on mission statements and detailed plans prepared by someone else. They have abandoned the command, compliance, and control approach that assumes that strategy formulation and execution take place in separate compartments. And they have abandoned the assumption that front-line managers cannot be trusted with the responsibility to think and act on the latest information in the best interests of the firm as a whole.

WHAT THEY HAVE PROMOTED. They have recognized that a clear governance framework provides the essential principles, values, and boundaries that enable front-line people to make decisions. They believe that it is the challenge, responsibility, and fairness of shared rewards that drive people to achieve extraordinary results. And they have adopted a "coach and support" management style that places performance responsibility on the shoulders of front-line people.

WHAT THEY HAVE GAINED. They have built a relative improvement contract based on mutual trust, with clear responsibilities for high-level performance from front-line people. They have also built a community spirit that reflects the interdependence of the organization and that supports seamless solutions for customers. Above all, they have recognized that people respond more positively to clear values and principles than to nebulous mission statements and detailed plans.

Creating a High-Performance Climate

WHAT THEY HAVE ABANDONED. The leaders mentioned earlier have abandoned an internal focus on negotiating financial numbers that fails to provide an external reality check on performance goals. They have abandoned the "management by fear" culture that puts people under intense pressure to meet fixed targets. And they have abandoned the process of negotiating fixed annual targets for each individual unit and subunit that fails to see them in the context of an integrated delivery system.

WHAT THEY HAVE PROMOTED. They have elevated peer-based performance reviews to a whole performance culture based on relative success. They have set high performance standards based on world-class benchmarks. Their aim is to be consistently at the top of their peer group. But they have also recognized the need to balance internal competition and cooperation by clarifying who owns which customer and by rewarding long-term value creation.

WHAT THEY HAVE GAINED. The result is a virtuous circle of high performance standards followed by sustained improvements. After a few years of catching up, both Ahlsell and Handelsbanken have since continuously set the standard in their industries. They have also been able to recruit and keep talented people, especially those who seek challenge and responsibility.

Providing Teams with the Freedom to Make Decisions

WHAT THEY HAVE ABANDONED. Leaders have abandoned the culture of dependency whereby local managers would always have to "go up the line" before a decision could be made. They have abandoned the cautious "safety-first" approach to strategy that leads to low expectations. And they have abandoned the exclusion of people from the strategy process on the assumption that only people at the center have the experience and wisdom to make good decisions.

WHAT THEY HAVE PROMOTED. Leaders have set high standards, expectations, and benchmarks to stretch ambition and performance. They have challenged local strategies and action plans to ensure they are sufficiently ambitious and robust at the same time, and that appropriate risks are taken. And they have opened up the strategy process to anyone who can make a contribution.

WHAT THEY HAVE GAINED. The benefits are that local people are more likely to produce imaginative strategies and are more committed to their successful execution. They are also better able to respond more rapidly to changing competitive conditions.

Focusing Performance Responsibility on Many Small Teams

WHAT THEY HAVE ABANDONED. Leaders have abandoned the assumption that business units and subunits should gradually increase in size to achieve greater economies of scale. They have abandoned the belief that the business should be organized around functions and departments within a top-down hierarchy. And they have abandoned the "macho manager" culture that celebrates individual winners and fails to recognize the importance of the interdependent team.

WHAT THEY HAVE PROMOTED. They have created and empowered many small units within the organization and given them the freedom to manage their own resources and be accountable for them retrospectively. They have recognized that the organization itself should be one interdependent team with a common purpose rather than a disparate collection of self-serving units. And they have celebrated the performance of the team over and above the individual.

WHAT THEY HAVE GAINED. They have built centers of excellence around the organization that have greater strategic and value creating capabilities than before. They have also reduced costs through fewer layers of management control.

Focusing People on Customer Outcomes

WHAT THEY HAVE ABANDONED. Leaders have abandoned the "plan, make, and sell" business model with central quotas and fixed sales targets that assumes that customers can be persuaded to buy what the firm decides to make. They have abandoned the belief that operating units serve the needs of the corporate center. And they have abandoned the "not invented here" syndrome that prevents units from sharing knowledge.

WHAT THEY HAVE PROMOTED. They have taken decentralization beyond major business units and down to the front line, enabling a network of small local teams to work within a clear framework of values and boundaries. They have encouraged a "can do" and "no blame" culture. Managers can do what needs to be done, and fix what needs to be fixed, knowing that there will be someone to support them if it doesn't work out. And they have inverted the organizational pyramid in which the center now serves operating units that, in turn, are focused on serving and satisfying customers' needs.

WHAT THEY HAVE GAINED. The result is greater personal accountability for outcomes and more satisfied and profitable customers. There is also more emphasis on providing value for customers rather than meeting an agreed upon plan.

Supporting Open and Ethical Information Systems

WHAT THEY HAVE ABANDONED. Leaders have abandoned the notion that information can be "controlled" when networks and e-mail enable it to flow round the globe in nanoseconds. They have abandoned the belief that the primary beneficiaries of information are people at the center. And they have abandoned the culture of "treating and spinning" information to make it represent an outcome that is divorced from reality.

WHAT THEY HAVE PROMOTED. They have promoted information flows at new levels of openness and transparency. They have given their people access to the sort of strategic, competitive, and market-based information that was once the preserve of senior executives. And they have understood that all the numbers within the organization should stick to "one truth." The numbers should be seen by everyone in their raw state without people "treating" them or painting pictures that are designed to mislead. This gives everyone confidence in the numbers and supports devolved decision making.

WHAT THEY HAVE GAINED. The outcome is more transparent and reliable information and more ethical reporting.

Scaling the Twin Peaks of Beyond Budgeting

Most of the companies we have visited started with limited objectives. Reducing the costs of budgeting and making the performance management process more relevant to its users were uppermost in their minds. In this sense they have scaled the first peak of beyond budgeting (see figure 2-1).

Staying with the mountaineering metaphor, it is only when they have reached this peak that many of them realized that the results would be more sustainable if they were supported by leadership actions that were more in tune with a radically decentralized organization model. This is what the next peak offers. This is not to say that these companies didn't achieve real benefits from reaching the first peak. Indeed, most organizations achieved significant cost savings, less gaming, faster response, better strategic alignment, and more value from the finance team.

FIGURE 2 - 1

The Twin Peaks of Beyond Budgeting

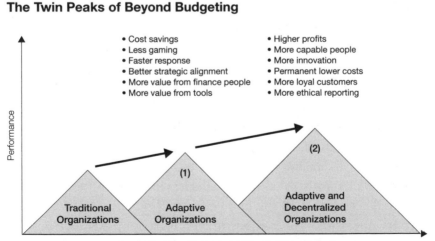

This last benefit was a surprise to many companies. For example, finance people are no longer seen as bean counters but as people who really help front-line managers with operational decisions. Moreover, the finance people are pleased with the results, as Borealis project leader Bjarte Bogsnes explains: "We now achieve what the planning and budgeting process did in a simpler, more direct way. In fact I would go further. The new system is not just simpler—it gives us far more information and control than the traditional budget ever did."

Leaders that saw the beyond budgeting opportunity in terms of radical decentralization believed that it would ultimately provide a significant competitive advantage. This was achieved by creating capable, committed, and empowered people at the front line. With the full power of information systems to provide them with the capabilities to make fast and effective decisions (unfettered by the budgeting counterculture), they can reduce costs, produce innovative strategies, create loyal and profitable customers, and provide more ethical reporting systems. Finally, these key value drivers lead to increases in shareholders' wealth based on sustained competitive success.

Transforming the performance potential of the organization by breaking free from the annual performance trap and releasing the full capabilities of front-line people is the ultimate vision of beyond budgeting. Implementing more adaptive management processes does not mean that project managers need to stray too far from their comfort zones. Devolving performance responsibility to front-line people, however, is more radical and needs strong and determined leadership from the top of the organization. But the potential benefits are far greater and more enduring.

Beyond Budgeting Provides Benefits for Shareholders

There are two primary issues facing investors in commercial companies today. One is whether they believe that an organization will produce sustainable growth in shareholders' wealth. The other is whether they trust the management team.

It is difficult to say categorically whether any one program of change (even with the benefit of hindsight) leads to a direct and measurable improvement in shareholders' wealth within a given period of time. It is easier to say what hasn't worked. For example, it is doubtful that many of the aggressive expansion projects of the 1990s involving significant mergers and acquisitions have improved the wealth of shareholders (except in the companies they acquired). But in a number of organizations that have migrated to the adaptive and decentralized model, their leaders have been adamant that it was this switch that underpinned their performance transformation. Here are six examples of how performance improved in the years following the change to the beyond budgeting model:

- *Carnaud Metal Box.* Under the leadership of Jean-Marie Descarpentries, this Anglo-French packaging company was transformed from a debt-laden company worth only $19 million in 1982 to a market value of $3 billion in 1989. By abandoning the fixed performance contract and encouraging business unit teams to set stretch targets (disconnected from a rewards system based on relative performance) he achieved what *Fortune Magazine* described as one of the best European corporate performances of the 1980s.
- *Groupe Bull.* Descarpentries was recruited from Carnaud Metal Box (CMB) to transform this French-government-owned mainframe computer company in the early 1990s. By deploying the same management principles that he used so successfully at CMB, the company turned around from losing F5.5 billion in 1993 to making a profit of F600 million in 1997, paving the way for a successful privatization.
- *Fokus Bank.* After abandoning the budgeting model in 1997, this small bank transformed itself from the worst performing bank in Norway with the highest costs to the best performing bank with the lowest costs and the highest return-on-capital-employed. Fokus Bank was acquired by Danish bank, Den Danske Bank, in 1999 at almost three times its flotation value four years earlier.
- *Ahlsell.* This Swedish wholesaler of heating, plumbing, refrigeration, and electrical products abandoned budgeting in 1995. A fast, open information system with a strong emphasis on relative performance now provides the necessary controls for self-governance by local units. Ahlsell is now the sector's most profitable company in Sweden in both of its main lines of business

(heating and plumbing, and electrical products)—a major turn-around from its position in the early 1990s.

- *Leyland Trucks.* This U.K. truck manufacturer had tried every improvement initiative from total quality to process reengineering but none of them led to improved performance. The difference came when CEO John Oliver abandoned piece work and the fixation with volume on the assembly line. In the first two and a half years after making these changes (from 1989 to 1991), the company reduced its operating costs by 24 percent (halving its breakeven level), and improved its return on sales to over ten percent (beating most of its European rivals). It was later sold to the U.S. company, PACCAR, to gain access to greater sources of development capital.
- *Svenska Handelsbanken.* Since abandoning the budgeting model in the 1970s Handelsbanken has produced outstanding returns for shareholders, consistently beating all its rivals in Europe on the key ratios of cost-to-income and costs-to-total assets. It is interesting how it communicates with investors. The CEO's annual message in the shareholder's report focuses on competitive performance. It shows a league table of cost-to-income and share price performance against its main competitors. It also spells out how its radically decentralized management model is a major source of competitive advantage.

Despite the case evidence, some investors may view the prospect of implementing beyond budgeting as a weakness rather than a strength. They will be concerned about the impact on management incentives and corporate governance. But such concerns are misconceived. If executive rewards are aligned with consistent competitive success rather than fixed contracts, then investors should be reassured that executives are focused on leading their industry peer group on a range of measures including those relating to shareholder value. (The SEC in the United States has recognized the need for relative measures at the executive level. It requires companies in their annual executive compensation disclosure to report the total returns to shareholders *relative to their peers or to the market as a whole.*)[10]

The other misconception is the belief that tight central (budgetary) control is an essential feature of well-governed organizations. This has surely been discredited by the events at Enron, WorldCom, Barings, and many other organizations that have been castigated for their abject failure to adhere to good governance and internal control practices. All these organizations had tight budgetary control processes that restricted information access to those that "needed to know."

Those organizations that have gone beyond budgeting have, to some degree or another, made their information systems more forward looking (using rolling forecasts), and far more open and transparent. This is a central part of improving governance and internal controls. If everyone sees the same information at the same time there is less opportunity for intermediaries to fudge the numbers. Nor do they have a reason to engage in such practices as there is no fixed target that must be met. It also places the CEO in a stronger position. As managers become more adept at preparing and interpreting rolling forecasts, the CEO is able to anticipate performance changes more effectively thus improving his or her ability to manage market expectations.

This approach should appeal to analysts. A leading U.S. analyst speaking at a recent BBRT meeting in New York made this point: "It is a huge mistake to predict the numbers. Analysts don't want fixed targets because things change. Nor are they overly interested in internal controls such as budgets. What they are interested in above all else is the company's ability to deliver sufficient amounts of free cash flows to support a growing dividend stream and share price." A new relationship between a company and its analysts is required. Rather than accepting earnings predictions from the CEO, the needs of the investor would be better served if analysts spent more time understanding the strategy and key value drivers of the business.

Swiss bank UBS provides a case in point. When the Union Bank of Switzerland merged with the Swiss Banking Corporation to form UBS in 1997 to form one of the world's largest banks, it made a number of commitments to the market, especially in terms of synergy-type cost savings. Indeed, it produced postmerger forecasts for the next five years that provided analysts with exactly what they wanted to see—growing profitability resulting from rationalization.

But such confident predictions, which effectively became a fixed performance contract based on detailed numbers, were to teach UBS a valuable lesson. Mark Branson, head of group communications at UBS, takes up the story:

> We provide very few financial performance commitments. Our experience shows they are counterproductive, building pressure for short-term action to save the credibility of forecasts. Now our aim is very much to build trust between the markets and the firm. We do this by being incredibly open. For example, we share a wealth of information on key issues such as strategy, value drivers, and key performance indicators, and provide detailed segmental reporting. In effect, we show analysts and investors how the business works. This shifts the emphasis from meeting short-term promises to improving our competitive position year after year. The result is much more accurate interpretation of our results and news flow, meaning less volatility in our shares. Analysts like and respect our approach. They no longer ask for numbers-based forecasts.

Replacing the budgeting process and fixed performance contract is the key to creating a more virtuous organization and building trust with investors. No one is promising an easy ride. Like all major change programs, the implementation process needs careful planning together with strong and consistent leadership. How information is used is crucial. If it is seen as a weapon of control, then the transformation process will be stillborn. If it is seen as a liberating tool for front-line managers to use their knowledge and judgment to respond responsibly and quickly to situations, then a new opportunity beckons. This is the approach taken by those organizations that have gone beyond budgeting.

- Abandoning the annual budgeting process opens up two opportunities. One is to enable a more adaptive set of management processes, and the other is to enable a radically decentralized organization. The first can be achieved without fully embracing the second, but the second cannot be realized without fully embracing the first.
- Succeeding at the first opportunity primarily concerns replacing the fixed performance contract with a relative improvement contract. This means that managers are expected to reach high competitive standards, but are then evaluated and rewarded after the event according to how they performed in the light of circumstances that actually prevailed and, perhaps more important, how they performed against their peers.
- Succeeding at the second opportunity concerns the ability of leaders to transfer power and authority from the center to operating managers, vesting in them the authority to use their judgment and initiative to achieve their goals without being constrained by some specific plan or agreement. This leads to greater motivation and achievement because it works with the grain of human nature rather than against it.
- Like the first opportunity (adaptive processes), the second opportunity (decentralization) can only be fully grasped if all the pieces come together in a coherent way. The result of fusing both opportunities together is the emergence of a new coherent performance management model.
- Creating the alternative coherent performance management model allows the full power of information systems and tools to be used. By removing the short-term budgeting counterculture, leaders are able to unblock systems and tools (e.g., the Balanced Scorecard) and open up the flow of knowledge to front-line people, thereby releasing the full potential of a radically decentralized organization.

- Using the principles of beyond budgeting to enable adaptive management processes does not mean that project managers need to stray far from their comfort zones. However, using them to enable the devolution of performance responsibility to front-line people is more radical and needs strong and determined leadership from the top of the organization.
- Beyond budgeting provides benefits for investors and strengthens corporate governance. The cost reduction opportunities alone are often sufficient to make a compelling case. Governance is strengthened through greater transparency and the eradication of the gaming practices that are so pervasive within many organizations today.

The Adaptive Process Opportunity: Enabling Managers to Focus on Continuous Value Creation

Chapter Three

How Three Organizations
Introduced Adaptive Processes

It is universally apparent that we are living in a
world so complex and so uncertain that authoritarian,
control-oriented companies are bound to fail.[1]
—GARY HAMEL

Part II explains the various ways that our case study organizations have replaced budgeting with alternative, more adaptive management processes. It does so in three chapters. This chapter explains what three organizations have actually done to replace the planning and budgeting process, chapter 4 draws a number of principles and best practices from these (and other) cases to outline the range of approaches taken and how they change behavior, and chapter 5 examines what we can learn from the implementation experiences of a number of organizations.

While the three cases featured in this chapter are representative of what most organizations have done, they are by no means the whole story. In chapters 4 and 5 we will provide many examples of how a number of U.S. and European organizations have taken the right steps in their efforts to implement adaptive processes (and experienced significant improvements) only to be thwarted by new owners or a lack of shared commitment at the corporate center.

The three organizations we have selected cover a range of industries and operate globally. They also range from a recent adopter to one company that has been managing without budgets for over thirty years.

- Rhodia is a French-based specialty chemical company with net sales of $7.2 billion, 27,000 employees, and 19 worldwide enterprises. It abandoned budgeting in 1999. It is a large and complex global organization that has developed a clearly defined methodology for replacing the traditional planning and budgeting process.
- Borealis is a Danish company that is now one of Europe's largest producers of petrochemicals, with sales of $4 billion. It abandoned budgeting in 1995. It is a company subject to rapid and unpredictable change.
- Svenska Handelsbanken is a Swedish bank with revenues of around $2 billion and 600 profit centers (mostly branches). It abandoned budgeting in 1972. This is a mature case involving a synthesis between new management processes and radical decentralization.

For each of these organizations, we provide some background and look at the reasons why they decided to replace the budgeting process, examine what they did, and then draw some conclusions. For each case, we examine the replacement processes through the six elements of budgeting: goals, rewards, action plans, resources, coordination, and controls.

Rhodia

Rhodia is one of the world's major specialty chemical companies. With its head office in Paris, it is now organized into five divisions that give the group its strategic vision and enable it to coordinate its nineteen worldwide enterprises that are focused on markets and customers and are responsible for their own results. They cover a wide range of consumer markets, including automotive, health care, fragrance, apparel, electronics, personal care, and environmental protection.

The Budgeting Problem

The old planning and budgeting process started in June and took around six months to complete. (In one year it wasn't completed until February!) It was based on an extrapolation from the past, and targets were subject to "adjustment" by operating managers. The result was little ownership or ambition. Nor was there any clear link with strategy. In fact, business management teams spent precious little time on strategy, and few understood how to manage the process. No one needed convincing that the budget provided poor value and should be replaced. The only concern was at the factory level, where a number of managers were used to working with predetermined plans and schedules that defined their work programs for the year ahead.

How the Annual Budgeting Process Was Replaced

Jacky Pinçon became leader of the "Spring" project and designed and developed an alternative performance management process (in conjunction with external consultants) to replace the annual budget. Its purpose was to improve group performance, clarify and communicate group strategy, and to develop a results based culture. Its key ingredients are discussed in the following subsections.

GOALS. Broad five-year goals (updated each year) based on return on capital and free cash flows are set out in an orientation letter from the group board to divisions, and from divisions to worldwide enterprises. These goals are derived from a mixture of industry benchmarks and an estimate of year-on-year growth potential for each division and enterprise. They set the framework for strategy reviews at every level.

REWARDS. Even in the old budgeting process, Rhodia did not link incentives to fixed targets, so a strict performance contract was never much in evidence. In the new process, managerial bonuses are evaluated with hindsight and paid on a line-of-sight basis, with an element based on personal results (40 percent) and an element based on business unit/enterprise/corporate results (60 percent). These evaluations occur every six months and are based on specific criteria related to strategic initiatives.

ACTION PLANS. There are now two performance management cycles (see figure 3-1). The first looks at medium-term goals and strategy (steering the business), and the second looks at short-term performance (managing the business).

The first step in the *medium-term strategy cycle* (S1) involves group executives setting broad five-year goals (return on capital expenditure [ROCE] expectations and rough capital expenditure parameters). These take into account the potential of the enterprise and drive the (rolling) five-year strategic plan. Managers then update the five-year plan annually. The second step (S2) involves managers reviewing the performance

FIGURE 3-1

Steering and Managing the Business with Adaptive Processes at Rhodia

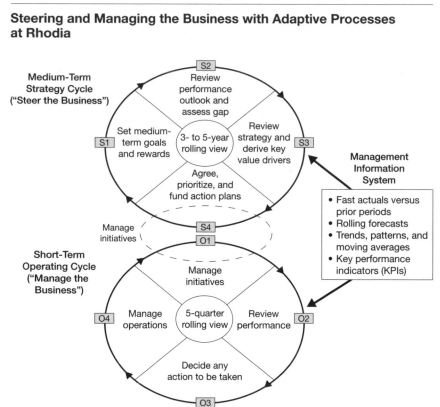

outlook and deciding whether further action is required to attain agreed-upon medium-term goals. Assuming that such action is required, they then get down to the task of reviewing strategy and identifying key value drivers (S3).

Performance reviews look at four perspectives:

1. *Strategic imperatives* take account of the corporate view.
2. *Strategic analysis* looks at markets and competitors.
3. *New challenges* take account of learning and growth.
4. *Performance analysis* looks at past and current trends.

The output is a short report with approximately one page devoted to each of these strategic perspectives. This report is the basis for a dialogue between the business team and senior executives who challenge the basis of planning hypotheses and their implicit risks and assumptions. This process is also part of the education program.

The final results of the strategic planning process are as follows:

- An agreed-upon set of four or five *key value drivers* such as "improve supply chain," "make acquisitions," "become number one in customer service," and "improve new product introductions." Each team produces a chart that shows the impact of its chosen key value drivers over the planning period. "Steady-state" adjustments (those that can be put down to "business as usual" changes in the market) are separated from the results of the selected key value drivers. This chart is, in effect, the road map for the future. It must be convincing and withstand serious questioning from senior people.
- A corresponding set of *strategic actions* for the next one or two years.
- A *business plan* showing financial forecasts (profits and cash flows) and capital expenditure.
- A detailed *cash analysis.*
- The *formulation of strategy* by the enterprise.

The fourth step (S4) is when each business team must produce around twenty to twenty-five strategic actions that will support its chosen key value drivers and be implemented over the next few years. The impact of each action plan must be shown on an "impact matrix" that indicates how a number of processes contribute to the achievement of each strategic action. This impact can be high, medium, or low. When completed, this matrix gives a complete picture of the resources demanded and whether or not these demands are realistic. This leads to the prioritization of actions and avoids potential bottlenecks such as overloading key people or information technology (IT) resources. It also helps to manage resources.

The first step in the *short-term operating cycle* (O1) is for managers to monitor existing initiatives. This is done by looking at the total impact of each action plan on sales, profits, and cash flows. Standard forms have been developed to capture forecast information and enable this information to be consolidated up the organization. Enterprises are encouraged to develop business models and leading indicators to improve the accuracy of the forecast process. The reporting system enables managers to measure the future impact of current action plans, compares forecasts with medium-term goals; the system also extrapolates and corrects any variances using "corrective action plans." Pinçon shared an observation on the action planning and rolling forecasting process:

> Forecasts and targets must be independent if we want to obtain both relevant action plans and reliable forecasts, allowing risks and opportunities to be identified and relevant corrective actions to be taken. They must not be produced for control purposes. Action plans must be focused on the "battlefields" where we can really act. There should be no "wishful thinking." It is also important to be realistic. Forecasts should reflect the fact that some businesses are cyclical and thus cannot always grow, even if this is "politically incorrect."

Actions are reviewed quarterly in line with rolling forecasts and quarterly results (O2). The third and fourth steps (O3 and O4) involve taking short-term strategic decisions such as changing prices, launching promotions, and generally managing the business.

RESOURCES. Outlined capital expenditure allowances are contained in the five-year orientation letters and goals. These cover a rolling five-year period, but they are not fixed. Additional capital is made available depending on the merits of the case. Within these parameters, the enterprise team can manage its own business. It is at this level that resources are related to key value drivers and action plans, and the strategic portfolio of initiatives is managed. If quarterly reviews show that a project is not meeting its objectives, it will likely be terminated and those resources released. The real strength of this approach is that resources are firmly related to strategic actions rather than functional or departmental budgets. This leads to less waste. Moreover, because decisions are made quarterly and within the orbit of the local management team, new business proposals are more likely to receive funding.

COORDINATION. The planning and resource management process defines the roles that each unit must play in supporting each strategic initiative. Rolling forecasts enable managers to regulate production activity within and across enterprises. The company has set up "user councils" through which services and prices for central and shared services are agreed upon. These are then charged to operating units on a variety of bases. These councils challenge performance and costs and thus help to maintain downward pressure on central costs.

CONTROLS. Management reports come in two formats. One is "cumulative actuals" compared with the same periods for the previous year. This is a monthly report. The other is the latest forecast compared with objectives (the five-year plan). This quarterly report also includes trends and moving averages. Budgets have been eliminated from the reporting process. The effect of these changes is to move performance management to a rolling quarterly review that looks at the short- and medium-term outlook in an integrated way.

Conclusions

Rhodia has shown what can be done in a large and complex global organization in a short time frame. Dismantling the budget, designing a new performance management methodology, and implementing this process in a top-down manner have been sufficient to galvanize this traditional organization into radical change. After three years, the new process is an acknowledged success. All enterprises and service units have defined their strategies. Most of them have action plans with quantifiable impacts. The forecasting process is well established and becoming increasingly accurate and relevant. And performance responsibility has been transferred from the center to business enterprises whose strategic capabilities are now improving.

Borealis

Borealis is one of the largest petrochemical companies in the world. Output from its products can be found in thousands of everyday products, from diapers, food packaging, and housewares to cars and trucks, pipes, and power cables. When it was formed in Denmark in 1994 as a joint venture between two Nordic oil companies (Statoil of Norway and Neste of Finland), it inherited most of its processes, systems, and people (including their mind-sets) from the various subsidiary companies of its Norwegian and Finnish owners. But to the management team, it felt like a new company in which a break with the past was not only seen as desirable but also as crucial to future success. Its new location in modern well-appointed offices in Copenhagen added to the sense of a fresh start with few managerial traditions to restrain its ideas and ambitions.

The Budgeting Problem

The major problem at Borealis was one of uncertainty. The petrochemicals industry is subject to well-defined but unpredictable business cycles that have a dramatic effect on performance. But the new company had other problems too. Benchmarking studies showed that it was a long way behind acceptable performance levels on such issues as costs and safety. This was the spur it needed to think more radically about how it should manage the business in the future.

Bjarte Bogsnes, VP of corporate control at the time, summed up the company's position:

> With so little control over input and output prices, forecasting within the industry is a lottery. You could be sure that as soon as the ink dried on the next year's budget that either input or output prices would change dramatically, making the whole exercise a complete waste of time. No one in Borealis needed too much persuading that the budgeting process added little real value and

should be dismantled. We wanted "more for less." But saying it is one thing—doing it is another!

How the Annual Budgeting Process Was Replaced

Project leaders decided to replace the functions of budgeting with a set of tools that included benchmarking, the Balanced Scorecard, activity accounting, and rolling forecasts. However, it was how they integrated these tools into a coherent performance management process that was the major difference.

GOALS. A range of high-level KPIs now sets the framework for goal setting within the company. Financial performance expectations, cost reductions, new product introductions, and customer satisfaction ratings are among many medium-term goals the company sets. Business units and sites are measured on return on capital employed *relative to the market*. This relative measure takes the impact of uncontrollable (and fluctuating) input costs such as feedstock prices out of the equation by measuring only improvements that managers can influence (for example, productivity and stock levels). Goals are based on a three- to five-year time frame and reviewed every year. It is up to business unit teams to interpret these goals within the context of their own businesses and to set their short- and medium-term targets accordingly.

As Bjarte Bogsnes explains, external benchmarking has played a key role in the goal-setting process:

> Targets are set in relation to either the competition or best practice. We do extensive benchmarking, both externally and internally, on everything from production to support costs. The benchmarking process also removes most of the internal negotiations. As soon as we have agreed with whom to benchmark, and where we should be compared to the benchmark, the target sets itself. And it is normally tougher than the old, internally negotiated, one. Few managers want to be laggards in fourth quartile.

REWARDS. The top thirty-five senior managers now have performance bonuses linked to KPIs. In fact, these bonuses now account for from 15 to 25 percent of total compensation. Of this bonus, approximately

50 percent is accounted for by the corporate Scorecard and 50 percent by the business unit/personal Scorecard. Each manager has a personal Scorecard that is used as an important element in the review. This is measured on a "180 degree" peer review system. These annual performance reviews can take place at any point in the year, given the rolling format of business reporting. Personal targets are also suggested by the individual and reflect the important issues within his or her sphere of influence.

ACTION PLANS. The approach adopted for achieving goals was described by Bogsnes as "tougher targets, greater freedom." By this he meant that in exchange for accepting tough targets, managers are freer to adopt their own solutions. They do this through the medium of the Balanced Scorecard. Its primary purposes are to address the drivers behind the financial figures, set medium-term targets and map and communicate the strategy, manage strategic initiatives, and report progress.

Scorecards are designed and developed at various levels. They focus on a number of strategic themes that are reviewed from time to time (usually annually). For example, the finance perspective is based on five objectives: return on capital, financing capability, geographic expansion, key markets leadership, and expense optimization. KPIs have been developed to support these objectives. Again, these are reviewed annually and have changed significantly in the period following the inception of the process. In the case of the financial perspective, the KPIs are currently "relative operating profit" and "total fixed costs."

RESOURCES. Although there is no capital budget as such, there are authority levels that can be used to approve investment decisions, depending on certain criteria. Investments are categorized into small, medium, and strategic. Only strategic investments require executive board approval. Every project should at least meet the company's cost of capital and be compatible with the strategic direction of the firm. If projects do need to be rationed because of cash constraints, then it is the hurdle rate that is adjusted, and priority is given to those projects with the highest return.

Borealis has been innovative in managing its fixed costs. By removing the budgeting floor mentality, project leaders recognized that the way was open to make significant inroads into these costs, many of which have traditionally been fiercely protected by some of the most powerful people in the organization. Bogsnes provides some further insight:

> Another learning we had was that although a budget can be a very effective ceiling for costs, it can be also an equally effective floor. Cost budgets tend to be spent whatsoever, even if they were approved based on 16- to 18-months old assumptions about why the costs/resources were needed (or were we the only ones starting the budget process in June of the previous year?). When we use cost targets now, they are more ambitious than before, but with much greater freedom in how to meet them.

Responsibility is devolved to operating managers who monitor trends within a medium-term target. No specific targets are set for costs (except for a "default" reduction level of between 0 and 2 percent) unless there is a step-change required. In the absence of such a step-change, costs are simply tracked on a monthly moving average (year-on-year) basis. This is an important part of the reporting system. Again there is no "micro" picture, just the broad-brush view of cost trends. Nor does this process require an annual review. It is a rolling system of cost management, which overcomes the "use it or lose it" mentality. The moving average picture is sufficient for most purposes. For example, it answers the broad questions, such as "Are costs under control?" and "Are they moving in the right direction?"

Another approach to managing costs was activity accounting. Bogsnes explains the Borealis approach:

> One of the tools to help us manage costs without budgets was more relevant cost-reporting using activity accounting. We were convinced we had low-hanging fruit by simply getting a better understanding of our costs. I have always seen it as a paradox that most companies record and report costs down to the last penny on what costs they incur (cost types) and who incurs these costs. But they record and report next to nothing on why these costs are incurred (for which activities or processes). This is the really important information to have, and this is how costs are described and discussed in our businesses.

COORDINATION. Borealis has invested heavily in an enterprise resource planning (ERP) system to drive the company toward working through processes and activities rather than through functions and departments. However, getting people to think and act like process owners was a tough challenge, and getting people to think like a team, as well as transforming attitudes and relationships at lower levels across the organization, is taking time. The ERP system is also enabling the company to manage the demand as well as the supply chain. Instead of fixing what will be made and sold at the start of the year, all supply processes now respond to actual demand as it arises. Rolling forecasts support monthly operating plans that help managers to estimate capacity and thus plan for any expansion or contraction.

CONTROLS. Business units produce Scorecards together with a two-page snapshot of performance that includes return on capital, a cost report (focused on moving averages), and some text that explains current performance and competitive issues. As a measure of how important the Scorecard has become inside the organization, board meetings look at Scorecard results *before* financial results.

Rolling five-quarter forecasts play an important role in the Borealis performance management process. Financial controller Thomas Boesen explains how they are compiled:

> Forecasts are updated quarterly and look five quarters ahead. They are a consolidation of individual spreadsheets that are gathered from all the responsibility centers in the company and thus are extremely useful for estimating year-end performance and planning tax payments and major capital expenditure programs. This approach has reduced dramatically the amount of time managers now spend in forecasting compared with the previous budgeting process. The reduction is about 95%. And because forecasts are separated from any form of performance evaluation and control, we get far more accurate forecasts than was ever the case with the budgeting system. I can't emphasize this point enough. If line managers are allowed to interfere with forecasts then you have little chance of getting an honest view. But it didn't happen immediately. A number of managers still included too many capital expenditure

TABLE 3 - 1

Borealis's Internal Accounting Presentation

Cost Center	Current Month	Same Month Last Year	Current Year-to-Date	Twelve-Month Moving Average	Percent Change— Moving Average over Last Year

proposals in their forecasts (otherwise they thought that they would lose them) until they realized that it made no difference to approval. Gradually they disappeared from the process; cash requirements were reduced; and the forecasts finally settled down at a much more realistic level.

Forecasts are used in conjunction with actual results to show trends for high-level KPIs such as return on capital, profitability, volumes, and so forth. These typically show the last eight quarters' actual results and the next five quarters' forecasts.

The monthly financial reporting system has also changed. The headings from a typical monthly report are shown in table 3-1. For each account, they show the current month's results compared with the same month for the previous year; the month-to-date cumulatives; a twelve-month moving average (thus smoothing out any monthly kinks); and the percentage change of the moving average over the previous year. This enables managers to see trends and take action if they are heading in the wrong direction.

Conclusions

There is now widespread acceptance of the changes to the budgeting process at Borealis. Apart from the recognizable benefits of absorbing little management time each year, the new approach helps managers to focus more on current competitive issues and look continuously for ways of improving the business. Some of its strategic goals, such as lowering the cost base and improving safety levels, have been met. The Borealis case also shows how the use of tools such as the Balanced Scorecard and rolling forecasts can help to manage the organization effectively without the need for annual budgets. However, Borealis has not achieved complete coherence. The reward system, for example, remains based on annual targets (though they cover a range of KPIs).

Svenska Handelsbanken

Though not large by international banking standards (it has 520 branches across the four Nordic countries and twenty offices in other major world centers), Handelsbanken offers a full range of financial services, supported by five product-based subsidiaries, including a mortgage company, a finance company, a life assurance business, a mutual funds business, and a telephone and Internet bank.

The Budgeting Problem

In the late 1960s the bank's performance had been poor. Its strategy was to be the largest bank in Sweden, and thus volume business was its declared aim. However, this led to high costs as a result of handling large numbers of small accounts and spending huge sums on marketing activities. A spectacular loss around the same time added to its woes. This was a time when banking was highly regulated, and Handelsbanken was in severe trouble with the authorities. It also had internal problems. Its centralized bureaucracy meant that it carried a heavy cost burden and that its decision making was slow, reducing the ability of branch managers to respond adequately to customer needs. In 1970 Dr. Jan Wallander was hired as CEO to turn the bank around.

Wallander's views about budgeting were influenced not so much by his intuition as by his rare depth of experience. His time as a professional economist and later as a non-executive director at Swedish electronics company L.M. Ericsson taught him that most planning and budgeting systems produce forecasts that fall into two types. First there is the "same weather tomorrow as today" version, in which case he notes, "Why bother to spend so much time making forecasts?" Second, there is the "different weather tomorrow from today" version, in which case "you haven't a hope of making accurate budgets and forecasts." Wallander noted that "either a budget will thus prove roughly right and then it will be trite, or it will be disastrously wrong and in that case it will be dangerous. My conclusion is thus: Scrap it!"

How the Annual Budgeting Process Was Replaced

Although Wallander's vision was to decentralize the business and empower front-line people, he realized from the outset that this could only be achieved by abandoning the top-down budgeting process. The replacement steering mechanisms that he introduced are set out in the following subsections.

GOALS. There is no discernible goal-setting process at Handelsbanken. Over the years the bank has used performance rankings based on a few KPIs to continuously improve performance relative to its rivals. So successful has this approach been that the bank now sets the world-class standard. Its challenge is to stay there. Regions and branches, in effect, set their own targets depending on the improvement step-change that they want to make. But managers equally know that this is a moving target because every other manager is trying to do the same.

Relative performance targets work at each level of the bank. At the group level, the bank aims to beat its rivals on its key measure of return on equity (ROE). At the regional bank level, regions compete with each other on ROE and on the cost-to-income ratio. And at the branch level, branches compete with each other on the cost-to-income ratio, on profit per employee, and on total profit. The most intense competition is at the regional bank level, where a cup is awarded each year to the winner. There is also a system of handicapping. Each year, capital is allocated to regions according to the Bank of International Settlements (BIS) rules (i.e., standard lending-to-capital ratios set according to the risk profile of the investment portfolio) and based on results of the last three years. The most successful region receives the highest capital allocation, thus making it harder to make a return in the following year. Similarly, the poorest performer receives the lowest capital allocation, thus making it easier for it to catch up.

Many people struggle to understand how branches both compete and cooperate with each other at the same time. One of the secrets is that while they strive to be the best at achieving low costs and high profits, they *do not compete for customers*. Each customer belongs to a specific branch, and all transactions (no matter where they take place) are routed back to that branch's profit and loss account. Another of the secrets is the reward system.

REWARDS. The staff bonus scheme supports competitive performance. Every year since 1973, the bank has allocated part of its profit to a profit-sharing system for employees. The funds are managed by the Oktogonen Foundation. The main condition for an allocation to be made is that the Handelsbanken Group must have a higher return on shareholders' equity after standard tax than the average for other banks, in accordance with the overall goal laid down for operations. The upper limit for the allocation is 25 percent of the dividend paid to shareholders. All employees receive the same allocated amount. Disbursements can be made when the employee reaches the age of sixty. Anyone who entered the scheme at its inception would have accumulated a fund value of around 3 million Swedish krona ($430,000) by 2000. Today, the Oktogonen Foundation is the bank's largest shareholder, with 10.2 percent of the voting power.

The profit-sharing system can only be understood in the context of its purpose. It is not intended to be an incentive for individuals to pursue financial targets; rather, it is intended as a reward for their collective efforts and competitive success. It might be called a "dividend" on their intellectual capital. Many people find it hard to understand the lack of financial incentives. Wallander's answer is that "beating the competition or one's peers is a far more powerful weapon than financial incentives. Why do people need cash incentives to fulfill their work obligations to colleagues and customers? It is recognition of effort that is important. Managers will only strive to achieve ambitious goals if they know that their 'best efforts' will be recognized and not punished if they fail to get all the way."

ACTION PLANS. Handelsbanken has been operating without budgets for over thirty years. Over that time trust and confidence have grown, and every opportunity has been taken to devolve more responsibility to operating managers. Branch managers at Handelsbanken really do "run their own business."

Magnus Lindskog is the manager of a medium-sized branch in Kista on the outskirts of Stockholm (Sweden's Silicon Valley), where one of the branch's customers, Ericsson, is the largest employer. He has twenty-five staff members and is responsible for the profitability of the branch. He explains how the process works:

We decide which of the bank's products to offer and at what price. Each year I prepare an informal work program—a rough action plan that sets the direction for the forthcoming period. I might discuss this with my regional manager, but it is not submitted to anyone as a formal action plan. It is merely a guide and is subject to constant review depending on the threats and opportunities that appear through the year. My staff are fully involved in the preparation of the work program and also have their own informal action plans that are reviewed every six weeks.

Building long-term customer relationships is the key focus of managerial attention. The bank's response to Internet banking is typical of this thinking, as Sven Grevelius, vice president of finance, explains:

> Unlike many other banks, we didn't respond to the Internet opportunity by creating a new business that was unconnected to the old as if customers wouldn't connect the two. Our strategy is based on finding and keeping the right customers and this applies just as much to Internet banking as in other parts of our business. The Internet is a way for both Handelsbanken and its customers to operate at lower costs. So we must, for example, make it easier and cheaper for them to pay bills on-line. As for more complex transactions such as loans and mortgages, we provide information but we still anticipate that customers will want to deal with a person rather than a computer system. We are a multi-channel bank and will continue to develop in this way. But our strategy remains intact. Customers are at the center and we will continue to take care of them no matter how they conduct their transactions with us.

RESOURCES. Because regions and branches know the KPIs that they must achieve, this defines the resources at their disposal. But to place continuous downward pressure on central services and make those services more responsive to market demands, Handelsbanken has developed an "internal market" that connects central service providers with internal customers. Sven Grevelius explains how it works:

> Staff departments should be faced with the necessity of "selling" their commodity to the rest of the organization and in competition

with outside suppliers if that is possible. While all central costs are allocated to profit centers such as regions and branches, they are not simply presented as a fait accompli. There is an annual round of negotiations whereby cost estimates and the services underpinning them are presented and discussed with all those involved.

Regional and branch managers have every right to challenge these costs and even reject them. It is an internal market where the central service "sellers" meet the business unit "buyers." Buyers check the prices against similar services in the marketplace and ensure that they receive value for their money. Central support departments are under constant pressure. This annual round involves real negotiation. A typical comment by a branch manager might be: "Since we are not increasing our costs, we expect you to do the same." Where possible, costs are attributed to branches on the basis of actual usage (e.g., by transaction, such as the number of mortgages or loans processed). However, all costs attributed to regions and branches are the actual costs to the bank. There is no internal markup or fudging of the numbers. In a decentralized performance model, the integrity of the numbers is crucial to success.

COORDINATION. The objective is to provide a fast, seamless solution for the external customer. To enable this to happen, Wallander abandoned central targets. Thus, there are no product targets or quotas that branch managers must meet. Fostering relationships across the organization is seen as the important element in creating coordinated actions. A strong commitment to a common set of values provides the framework for this process. Everyone thinks about the customer. Product development is modular. In other words, products (and parts of products) can be used as building blocks to respond to customer requests.

Sven Grevelius provides an example of how IT is delivering faster service and lower costs by enabling branches to offer customized life assurance policies:

> The new life assurance policy introduced in 1997 can include an old-age pension, a family pension, and accident and sickness insurance, depending on the needs of the customer. This policy

can be taken out in any branch, tailored to customer needs, prepared on site, and presented to the customer before he or she leaves. In other words, there is no further processing; the policy is valid and all the work is completed before the customer leaves the branch. This is just one example of how we meet the changing needs of customers.

CONTROL. Handelsbanken focuses on only a few key measures that are deeply embedded throughout the organization. Return on equity, cost-to-income ratio, profit per employee, and total profitability are simple measures that apply at every managerial level and define the firm's competitive position.

It also relies more on "fast actuals" than predictive information. Its ability to monitor tens of thousands of transactions a day and extract valuable knowledge from the changing patterns of customer acquisitions, defections, and discounts is testament to its competence in this area. Though rolling cash forecasts are prepared each quarter, they are given low visibility. In fact, they are only seen by the CEO and the vice president of finance. These forecasts inform the CEO of the likely quarterly results. They also provide an early warning that cash flows are starting to improve or decline, and thus help to plan investment and liquidity requirements. They are prepared by the finance department and based on current trends and on short phone calls with key people. The amount of resources spent in preparing them over a year is probably no more than about a quarter of one person.

Current Chairman Arne Mårtensson has said that the bank replaced the budget with "an excellent accounting system." This means that it is fast, open, and delivers relevant information to the right people at the right time. Group controller Ulf Hamrin explains what this means at Handelsbanken:

> Too many senior managers seem to accept that obtaining fast information is beyond their reach. These people don't know what they're missing. The problem is not lack of investment. It is caused by a poor understanding of what users require. We have spent many years fine-tuning our management information system so that every manager receives exactly what is required both for his or

her own decision-making purposes and to stay in touch with the wider aspects of the organization. Speed is of the essence. Our branch managers know the cost of every proposed transaction and can see what's happening across the customer base at any time. We at head office can also monitor this information but we don't use it to undermine the authority of the local manager. These are the checks and balances that make our system work. Managers know that we know what's going on, but they equally know that they have the freedom to make decisions and fix problems without interference.

As one might expect, risk management is also an important part of the performance management system at Handelsbanken. Hamrin, as group controller, is able to view branch and regional balance sheets each day and assess their risk exposure. He can see patterns of loans and investments and view the risk profile across the portfolio.

Conclusions

By abandoning budgeting and embracing new adaptive processes, Handelsbanken has developed a mature and stable performance management process. Its key principles of "beat the competition," performance-league tables, shared rewards, customer ownership, "can do" decision making at the front line, and a few easy-to-follow relative measures have been the hallmarks of its sustained success.

Chapter Summary

- This chapter described how three organizations have replaced budgeting with alternative adaptive management processes.
- Rhodia abandoned budgeting in 1999. Its aim was to implement more relevant and useful processes. It now uses a short- and medium-term performance management cycle to monitor progress and decide on further action.
- Borealis abandoned budgeting in 1995. It replaced the budgeting process with a set of tools that included benchmarking, the Balanced Scorecard, activity-based management, and rolling forecasts. Almost immediately, the focus of management attention was switched from the financial accounts available to a select few to KPI-based charts posted on open Web sites and office walls.
- Svenska Handelsbanken abandoned budgeting in 1972. This is a mature case involving a synthesis between adaptive management processes and radical decentralization. Its results have been extraordinary.

Chapter Four

Principles of Adaptive Processes

If you *cannot* know what your customers will want or your
competitors will offer next year—or even who your customers
or competitors will be—you cannot develop an effective plan
for achieving targeted levels of sales and profits.[1]
—STEPHAN HAECKEL

The three cases described in chapter 3 can tell us much about the principles and practices of managing with adaptive processes as opposed to
annual budgets. Although their approaches have been similar, they have
not been the same. The primary purpose of this chapter is to identify
and explain the key principles that best describe what they have done.
Then we will examine how these alternative processes change attitudes
and behavior.

Six Principles of Managing with Adaptive Processes

It is clear from the approaches adopted by our cases that breaking free
from the fixed performance contract is the key to unlocking stretch targets, implementing adaptive processes, and eradicating most of the
undesirable game playing that pervades the budgeting process. The six

principles of managing with adaptive processes examined in this section are as follows:

1. Set stretch goals aimed at relative improvement.
2. Base evaluation and rewards on relative improvement contracts with hindsight.
3. Make action planning a continuous and inclusive process.
4. Make resources available as required.
5. Coordinate cross-company actions according to prevailing customer demand.
6. Base controls on effective governance and on a range of relative performance indicators.

The results of applying these principles can be seen in figure 4-1. These include setting aspirational goals, reducing gaming, encouraging ambitious strategies and fast response, reducing waste, improving customer service, and promoting learning and ethical behavior.

FIGURE 4 - 1

Beyond Budgeting Principles Enable a Continuous Adaptive Process

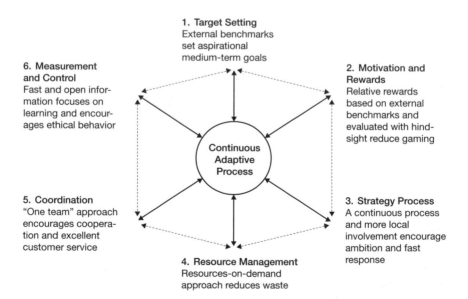

1. **Target Setting**
External benchmarks set aspirational medium-term goals

6. **Measurement and Control**
Fast and open information focuses on learning and encourages ethical behavior

2. **Motivation and Rewards**
Relative rewards based on external benchmarks and evaluated with hindsight reduce gaming

Continuous Adaptive Process

5. **Coordination**
"One team" approach encourages cooperation and excellent customer service

3. **Strategy Process**
A continuous process and more local involvement encourage ambition and fast response

4. **Resource Management**
Resources-on-demand approach reduces waste

The following sections examine the principles in more depth. For each principle, we also set out a range of options that project teams have used to apply it in their organizations.

Principle 1: Set Stretch Goals Aimed at Relative Improvement

Whereas most organizations still set goals based on annually negotiated internal targets, our featured organizations prefer to set goals based on maximizing their short- and long-term performance potential. In some cases, these aspirational goals are disconnected from performance evaluation and rewards. In other cases, there is a direct connection between goals based on relative measures and how performance is evaluated and rewarded. However, in neither case is there a fixed performance contract based on a fixed target agreed upon in advance.

SET "STRETCH" GOALS DISCONNECTED FROM PERFORMANCE EVALUATION AND REWARDS. Some leaders have used the abandonment of fixed targets to say to their business unit teams, "What can you really do if you try?" In other words, they have not set lower or upper limits on what is expected or possible. The onus is on the team to set their own goals based on their highest aspirations. However, it is *crucial that the stretch goal is not seen as a fixed target against which performance will be evaluated.*

Jean-Marie Descarpentries was a successful practitioner of this approach when he was in charge of the Anglo-French packaging company Carnaud Metal Box in the 1980s, and the French computer maker Groupe Bull in the mid-1990s. His success in both cases was based on a belief in separating target setting from performance evaluation and rewards.

Each business unit team had to propose its own stretch target. This was a projection of the "best possible outcome" on the basis of everything going right, including maximum demand and new products being launched on time. But then—and this was the key to his approach—Descarpentries would promptly forget about the targets. "The purpose," he noted, "is to get managers to dream the impossible dream." He didn't measure managerial performance against the target (thus creating a fixed performance contract), because in that case managers would not enter into the spirit of the stretching process. Instead, he evaluated and rewarded his managers on a range of indicators including how they performed this year versus last year and how they performed against the competition (this is explained further in principle 2). The purpose of the target was to drive imaginative strategies that lifted performance above and beyond incremental change. In other words, managers had to use their judgment and take risks.

SET GOALS RELATIVE TO EXTERNAL BENCHMARKS. Once external benchmarks are agreed upon, there is little need for negotiation. Performance is continuously evaluated based on the progress made against the benchmarks. Benchmark goals tend to be based on industry best-in-class performance measures or direct competitors, and teams are given an extended period of time to reach them. They are not specific annual targets. Most companies set their sights on consistently being in the top quartile of their peer group. Typical KPIs include return on equity and cost-to-income ratio. Bulmers, Borealis, and Rhodia have all used this approach.

It was also used successfully by U.S. eye care company, CIBA Vision. Its objective was to shorten and simplify the budgeting process and to reduce the amount of "budget gaming" by basing targets (with little negotiation) on competitor and market performance. CIBA Vision also developed internal relative measures and produced an (informal) ranking of them in internal league tables to show the performance of different companies based on sales growth or asset turnover. When first published, these internal league tables led to animated discussions among those whose performance was below average or worse than they had expected. It was a very useful spur to improving performance and it started a more active interchange of best practices within the company.

SET GOALS RELATIVE TO INTERNAL PEERS. Another (similar) approach is to base goals not on specific benchmarks but on continuously improving relative performance against internal peers. They should preferably be based on the KPIs that drive competitive success within homogeneous business units across a group. Operating teams at both Handelsbanken and Ahlsell set their own improvement goals based on what they think is needed to improve their position in their peer group performance rankings table. The design of the accounting system is key to ensuring that the measures are comparable across units.

Peer group league tables might be based on regions, countries, branches, plants, and service centers, as well as portfolios of customers, products or services. The objective is to create performance-league tables at every level that are coherent with the organization's strategic goals. Even if not directly comparable, some common measures based on, for example, efficiency, quality, and safety can usually be found. The pressure that arises from a unit's position in the league table drives continuous improvement. Although "relative" benchmarks can of course go down as well as up, all firms set high standards that managers are expected to achieve. Even the lowest-quartile performers at Handelsbanken would outscore most of the top-quartile performers at rival banks.

Principle 2: Base Evaluation and Rewards on Relative Improvement Contracts with Hindsight

The evidence from our cases suggests that there are different ways to align rewards with performance, all of which avoid forming fixed performance contracts. One focuses on the relative success of teams based on a range of KPIs, another is based on an individual receiving a bonus package with elements related to the performance of different units (e.g., business unit and corporate), and yet another involves disregarding all lower-level reward systems and opting for a groupwide profit-sharing scheme. Each organization has handled rewards in a different way. However, the common principle is that they do not link rewards to fixed targets agreed upon in advance.

BASE REWARDS ON THE RELATIVE SUCCESS OF OPERATING TEAMS. While "pay for performance" remains the underlying principle in deciding salaries and bonuses, the most common approach for the bonus element has been to agree on a relative improvement contract that involves a whole team (not individuals) setting and meeting a range of performance benchmarks over a period of time. Performance is then evaluated by a peer review group (using relative measures) with the benefit of hindsight. Although managers know in advance which KPIs they will be assessed on and what constitutes "acceptable performance" (or the "benchmark expectation"), they generally don't know until the end of the year how well they have performed and thus how much bonus they will receive. Because performance is evaluated against a range of factors relative to competitors, the market, and maybe the previous period, managers also know that they can achieve good bonuses in a low-profit year (though affordability may be a factor) and poor bonuses in a high-profit year, depending on their relative performance. The relevant question that the peer review panel must ask is: "Did they do as well as they could have done given what we now know about the profit-making opportunities during the period and what the competition has achieved?"

It is the uncertainty that drives success. It is like a car race in which each driver has to beat the competition while at the same time dealing with many unknown factors that will determine the outcome, such as the performance and behavior of other drivers, the reliability of the car, and the weather conditions. Each driver roughly knows what has to be done prior to the race to improve his or her usual performance and preferably win. But only with hindsight will the drivers know how well they have performed. This "relative performance" approach focuses business unit managers on maximizing profits at all times rather than playing games with the numbers, because there are no fixed targets that lead to irrational behavior. The downside is that because there is no fixed target against which to evaluate performance, the level of the bonus is decided by peer reviews that are invariably subjective. However, most firms have used a formula to provide some structure to these reviews and an appropriate mix of peer reviewers. Table 4-1 shows a typical formula.

Table 4-1 is similar to the formula used by Descarpentries at Groupe Bull in the mid-1990s. As we noted earlier, each business unit team set its goals knowing that they would not be measured directly against them. It would be this formula *based on relative KPIs* that would be used. Each KPI was given a weighting according to the degree of difficulty (rather like a diving competition). At the end of the year an executive committee would evaluate performance and mark each KPI out of one hundred. The weighted score for each KPI was then produced and the aggregate of the weighted KPI scores was the final result.

How the final scores were applied to individual bonuses is interesting. Here is how it worked: Maximum performance bonuses were set at 30 to 50 percent of salary at the executive level, 20 to 30 percent at the

TABLE 4 - 1

Performance Appraisal Formula for a Business Unit Using a Relative Improvement Contract

Key Performance Indicator	Weighting	Total Score	Weighted Score
Growth versus previous year	20	50	10
Growth versus competition	20	40	8
Profit versus previous year	20	60	12
Profit versus competition	20	50	10
Debt versus previous year	10	80	8
Quality factors versus previous year	10	60	6
Executive Committee Evaluation			**54%**

operating level, and less (although not zero) in other areas. But what was interesting was how the actual payout was calculated. Take a business unit. If a business unit employee had a base salary of $50,000 and the maximum bonus was set at 30 percent (or $15,000) and the formula set the payout at 60 percent, then the final payout would be $9,000. Both the corporate president and his executive committee independently review performance. First they examine growth versus last year and against the competition, bearing in mind all the competitive factors that pertained during the period. Second, they examine profitability. Third, they look at debt. Finally, they look at certain qualitative factors such as employee turnover. The choice of balance sheet and strategic measures might be different for each business unit. This assessment sets the bonus levels of all managers and employees within that particular business unit. If a business unit team underperforms, it is given a second chance. But if it underperforms again the following year, the team members are likely to be moved elsewhere or even receive dismissal notices.

Camille de Montalivet, ex–finance director of Groupe Bull, explains the system's goals as follows:

> The whole point about the evaluation process is that it is seen to be fair and is detached from both target setting and forecasting. Also the components and weightings of the formula are cleverly thought

out. With a strong bias toward growth, managers cannot simply "make their target" by cutting discretionary expenditures such as training, marketing, and satisfaction programs. And with the inclusion of qualitative factors (that can be any measures closely related to the needs of the business unit), there is a built-in assurance that managers will spend considerable effort on continuously improving the business. At senior levels of the organization, managers might have only part of their bonus linked to a business unit's performance and part linked to the group result. I cannot emphasize enough how important these reward systems were in the performance transformation at Groupe Bull.

BASE REWARDS ON MULTILEVEL PERFORMANCE. Companies such as Rhodia and Borealis use multilevel performance as a basis for individual rewards. At Rhodia, for example, managers receive a bonus payout resulting from their personal performance appraisal, the performance of their business unit, and the performance of the firm as a whole. Borealis adopted a similar approach for senior managers using the Balanced Scorecard to select the KPIs that would be applied to the bonus formula.

BASE REWARDS ON THE RELATIVE SUCCESS OF THE GROUP. Handelsbanken uses only one groupwide profit-sharing scheme for all employees. Thus, there are no set incentives for any team or salesperson to achieve a specific target. Nor are branches rewarded for their placement in the performance-league table (although they are *recognized* in different ways, thus increasing the importance of league tables). The bank uses the language of gain sharing (sharing in the fruits of collective success) as opposed to individual incentives (you must achieve x result to earn y bonus) to provide people with a stake in the success of the organization. Handelsbanken executives believe that its groupwide profit-sharing scheme is an important element in removing the cellular or "defend your own turf" mentality that pervades many organizations. It avoids the problem of rewards becoming entitlements that, if not received, lead to a disaffected and, in some cases, a demoralized workforce.

The important issue is not so much the financial payout but the *recognition* of the contribution that employees make to the organization's success. This case debunks the idea that direct financial incentives are necessary to reinforce performance improvement. Wallander believes that as far as motivation is concerned:

> [W]e find that our people are driven by their urge to show a better result than their competitors—to be above average. The Oktogonen profit sharing scheme in which every employee has an interest is also important. Essentially, motivation is based on the self-satisfaction of doing a good job for the company and the praise they will get. We have no specific proof of this, but it's what we believe and we think the evidence shows up in the results.

Handelsbanken operates with multilayered league tables of like branches and regions that appear every month, maintaining a strong focus on performance and harnessing the power of peer pressure.

Some people might argue that moving incentives away from individual performance is a charter for producing free riders—those managers who keep out of the limelight yet produce little by way of results. The experience at Handelsbanken, however, suggests that this is not as big a problem as feared. In a team-based organization driven by peer pressure, free riders are exposed very quickly and replaced by people more willing to commit themselves to real performance challenges.

Principle 3: Make Action Planning a Continuous and Inclusive Process

One of the clearest observations from reviewing the three cases in chapter 3 is that while the calendar or fiscal year might be an appropriate time period for reporting results to investors, it is unlikely to be an appropriate time period for managing the business. It neither fits with strategic initiatives, which normally go beyond the one-year budget period and often involve multiple business units, nor with economic or business cycles, or other unforeseen events. Moreover, it can (and often does) cause dysfunctional and disruptive behavior as managers scramble to meet their targets at the end of every period.

It is apparent from our cases that the planning process is devolved to at least the level of major business units. Another key change is that managers focus on creating value for customers and shareholders rather than on negotiating numbers and following a predetermined plan. Indeed, in the absence of a single plan that determines their actions for the year ahead, managers become much more aware of their changing business environment and are more prepared to face different possible scenarios.

DEVOLVE STRATEGY TO BUSINESS UNIT TEAMS. Though strategy and performance responsibility is devolved from the corporate center to teams closer to the customer, group executives still have an important role to play in the development of strategy. For example, they set values, boundaries, direction, and guidelines for strategy development and decision making, and then challenge the plans and ambitions of business unit managers. This process is done in broad strokes, and quickly. There are few detailed submissions and presentations. The only exception is if new capital expenditures or other major resource requirements are needed to support strategic options.

The extent to which the strategy process is devolved depends on a number of factors, including the culture of the business and the capabilities of lower-level teams. Different leaders have taken different approaches to the strategy process. One group of leaders have released central control slowly and relied more on methodologies and models (e.g., the Balanced Scorecard) to implement their new processes and systems. Senior executives take a more hands-on approach to planning as they agree on stretch goals and monitor key value drivers and strategic initiatives. Planning typically follows two cycles. One is a medium-term strategic cycle with annual reviews, and the other is a short-term operating cycle with quarterly reviews. Organizations that operate in the manufacturing and process industries tend to have followed this approach. Borealis and Rhodia (both mixtures of manufacturing and process businesses) are exemplars. At Volvo they also used a long-term (ten-year) planning cycle as well as a medium-term (four-year) strategic cycle, both with annual reviews.

Another group of leaders has focused on the devolution of performance responsibility to large numbers of profit centers and relied on peer-to-peer competitive league tables to drive continuous performance improvement. Senior executives take a hands-off approach to planning, leaving improvement initiatives to local teams. Planning is informal and continuous as teams constantly watch for signals that indicate a change of direction. Managers tend to use few tools, preferring to rely on fast and open information systems to monitor performance. Major investment proposals are dealt with as they arise. Service and distribution companies tend to have followed this approach. Both Handelsbanken (a bank) and Ahlsell (a wholesaler) are exemplars.

FOCUS ON CONTINUOUS VALUE CREATION.   One of the primary benefits of managing without a predetermined plan or budget is that managers are able to focus all their attention on responding to changing events and providing value to customers and shareholders. Figure 4-2 shows how this continuous performance review process can work. As we noted earlier in the chapter, this process can be structured around calendar reviews or be reviewed continuously by teams who respond to

FIGURE 4 - 2

The Continuous Performance Review Process

Process Controls
- Governance principles and ethical values
- Strategic and KPI boundaries
- Risk management (senior management challenges planning hypotheses and risks)
- Actual results, KPI reports, trends, league tables, and rolling forecasts

Process Inputs
- Organization/BU vision
- BU strategic direction and customer value proposition
- High-level, medium-term HO/BU goals and "baseline" expectations
- Small high-level KPI set
- Rewards policy

Performance Review Process
- Review performance outlook and assess gap
- Review and reset high-level goals
- Review strategy and key value drivers
- Agree, prioritize, and fund action plans
- Coordinate plans across the business
- Review KPI targets and controls

Process Outputs
- Agreed strategy
- Agreed "execution" list of action plans
- KPI set
- Revised rolling forecasts (showing impact of action plans on profit and cash flow projections)

Process Resources
- Support from senior managers and centers of expertise
- Tools (e.g., Balanced Scorecards and shareholder value models)
- Information on competitors, market intelligence, and economic indicators

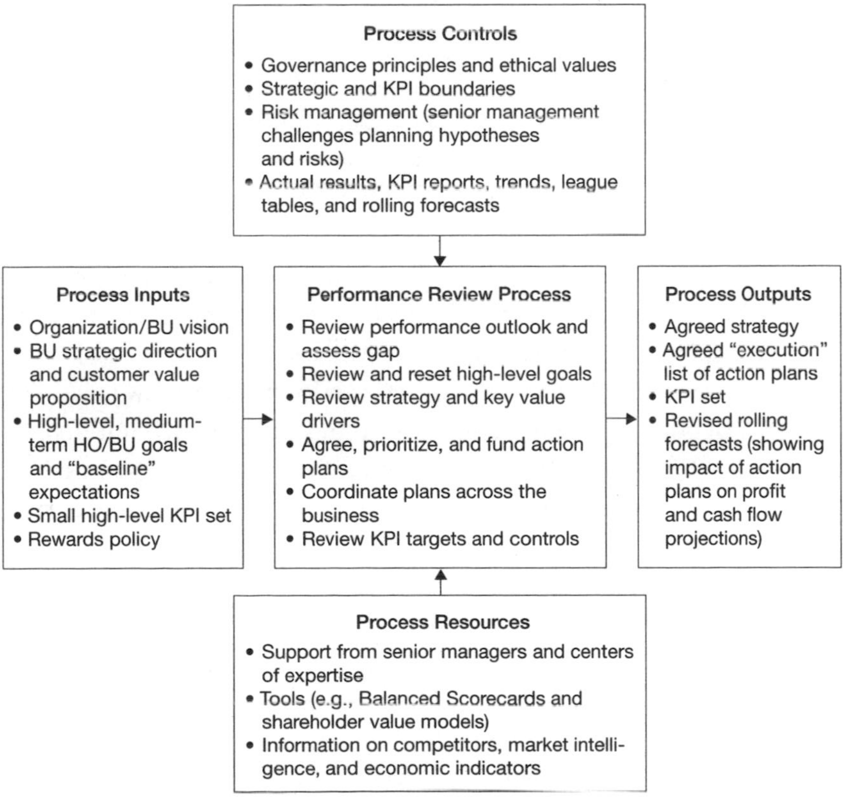

change as appropriate. The process is explained in more detail in the following section starting with the outputs followed by inputs, then the review process itself, and finally the controls and resources that make the process more rigorous.

- *Outputs.* The objectives of the review process are to produce an agreed upon strategy that the team can communicate to all sub-unit teams, an agreed upon list of action plans that project teams can execute, a KPI set that can form a framework for subsidiary KPI sets, and a revised rolling forecast showing the impact of the action plans on future profit and cash flow projections.

- *Inputs.* The performance review process will be conducted with the benefit of a number of important parameters relating to the broader organization and leadership context. For example, managers will take into account the organization (or business unit) vision that states its purpose and long-term goals. They will be aware of the strategic direction and the chosen customer value proposition for the business unit. These are significant inputs to the strategy and key value driver parts of the review process. They will also be aware of the expectations of higher-level management both in terms of stretch and baseline medium-term goals. These should be adjusted to reflect the current reality (e.g., they should take account of business cycles and competitive performance). There will also be a few KPIs that will be used to evaluate (and likely reward) their performance (e.g., ROCE). Finally, they will know how they will be rewarded.

- *Performance Review Process.* The performance review process will normally occur at a predetermined frequency, but it may also be triggered by a significant event or external change. It should begin with an examination of the performance outlook and assess the gap between the current trajectory and the (adjusted) medium-term goals. To make this assessment, managers need access to a complete information picture. This should include current actuals, competitive performance, trends, moving averages, leading indicators, and market intelligence. They must then estimate where "business as usual" will take them and compare this projection with where they want to be.

If there is a future performance gap then a strategic review will be triggered. This can be minor (just a one or two initiatives are required) or major (the performance gap is growing and a serious strategic review is required). Indeed, there will always be a time for a major strategic review when the "big" questions are addressed. Have the needs of our customers changed? Are our products and services still appropriate? Is our value proposition still valid? Do our chosen value drivers and KPIs still reflect the way that value is driven in the business? Do our core competences still support the value proposition? Do we need to take action to counter competitive threats and take sudden opportunities? These are the questions that a full strategic review should answer. In most businesses they only need to be addressed every two to five years, but in fast changing markets, they may need to be addressed much more frequently.

Having determined whether a minor or major strategic initiative is required, managers must now agree to the actions that can deliver the desired results. The right people need to be involved and, in some cases, this will be more than senior management. It should include all operational managers and any "activists" that can make a serious contribution. Ideally, managers should be looking for a portfolio of strategies that deliver both revenue growth and cost and productivity improvements. Strategic ideas might start as flashes of inspiration but they soon require hard evidence to support their underlying assumptions. And with hundreds of initiatives becoming common in many large companies, common formats and templates are needed to collate and present information.

Once the strategic review has been completed, managers should have identified the initiatives that will meet their strategic objectives. Once they have been agreed upon, strategic initiatives need to be approved and funded. This is rarely a straightforward process. Teams need to consider scarce resources and potential bottlenecks (e.g., IT resources). They must also work within agreed resource parameters and, in the case of major resource requirements, submit proposals to a higher approval level. Action plans are invariably cross-functional; thus they need to be project managed and coordinated with units across the organization.

Finally managers must consider and choose a set of KPIs that underpin their value drivers and action plans. These KPIs provide the detailed goals and controls that enable managers at all levels to monitor business performance.

- *Controls.* The team will also need to work within clearly stated governance principles and ethical values. Strategic and KPI boundaries are another constraining parameter. These can be used to guide managers in how much of a resource is available (e.g., marketing expenditure might be agreed on a percentage of sales). The team will need to discuss its proposed strategy and action plans with senior executives and answer their questions regarding choice of plans and implicit risks. It will also look at a wide range of performance measures including actuals, leading indicators, league tables, and rolling forecasts.
- *Resources.* The team will also need support. Providing the right education, coaching, information, and, in some cases, tools, can make the difference between success and failure. Identifying key value drivers and preparing strategy maps that link financial goals to operational changes is no easy task. Tools such as Balanced Scorecards, shareholder value models, and activity-based costing models can help teams to understand these links and derive appropriate action plans and KPIs. However, they should be used *by the team to support their strategy decisions and not by senior executives to control performance.* Teams also need fast access to the sort of information (e.g., intelligence on competitors and markets) that was previously the province of senior executives.

Principle 4: Make Resources Available as Required

All our cases have recognized that if performance responsibility is to be transferred to operating managers, then these managers need fast access to resources. Access to operating resources such as people and technology can be provided through a number of mechanisms, including KPI parameters, an internal market for operational resources, fast-track approvals for major projects, and devolving approval authority for smaller projects.

PROVIDE KPI PARAMETERS WITHIN WHICH TO OPERATE. In most cases leaders have provided their operating managers with guideline financial ratios based on KPIs to define the parameters within which they can commit resources (e.g., a cost-to-income ratio). Within these boundaries, managers have wide discretion over how they utilize their resources. These ratios perform the self-regulatory control functions of budgets. However, unlike budgets, they allow managers more scope and flexibility in how resources are deployed.

PROVIDE AN INTERNAL MARKET FOR OPERATIONAL RESOURCES. Another way of making resources available on demand is through an internal market. In this way operating managers are able to decide on the central services they need and commit to a service-level agreement with service providers. However, the important change is one of *relationship* because operating units become customers of service providers, with needs that must be satisfied. These agreements should require service providers to satisfy their customers' changing demands while at the same time adjusting their resources dynamically (i.e., not just once a year).

PROVIDE FAST-TRACK APPROVALS FOR MAJOR PROJECTS. Although some business units within the cases we have featured have some capital expenditure discretion, serious expenditure is still applied for through a capital expenditure application/approval procedure. However, to prevent this being an annual cycle, these expenditures can be approved as and when required.

DEVOLVE APPROVAL AUTHORITY FOR SMALLER PROJECTS. Small investments are generally handled within approval levels. For example, Borealis does not allocate a capital budget as such, but there are authority levels that can be used at any time throughout the year depending on certain criteria. The investment portfolio is integrated with rolling forecasts, and regular analyses are made up of past investments, approved investments, and pipeline investments, resulting in a better system of prioritization.

Principle 5: Coordinate Cross-Company Actions According to Prevailing Customer Demand

For most organizations, the master budget defines the financial commitments that one process team makes to another for the year. However, when managing without budgets, no such plan exists, so managers must

coordinate these commitments according to the pace of market demand. The trade-off is that although fixed capacity may not be fully uti-
lized (e.g., the "make for stock" approach), there is less waste (with fewer
write-downs) and more satisfied customers (whose exact requirements
are more likely to be met). The approaches taken by our cases include
providing customized solutions, managing short-term capacity in real
time, and managing customer profitability information.

PROVIDE CUSTOMIZED SOLUTIONS. Responding to unanticipated customer requests might involve one or more business units together with
one or more service providers—and some of these providers can be
external suppliers. Thus, some of the cases we reviewed are beginning to
operate more like consultancies. Handelsbanken has moved toward this
approach through its ability to offer customers highly tailored solutions
by "snapping together" modular products.

MANAGE SHORT-TERM CAPACITY IN REAL TIME. In the traditional
model, budgets are used to fix capacity well in advance, thus determining much of the product cost before the first unit is made. Standard costing is then used to monitor efficiency variances that encourage the
recovery of all direct overheads, no matter what the consequences might
be for quality or other hidden costs (e.g., high or unsaleable inventories)
of the finished output. In organizations that have abandoned budgets,
market-facing business units become customers of upstream processes
and central service providers, and suppliers to external customers. The
ultimate objective is to match resource needs to prevailing customer
demand.

At Bulmers, for example, it quickly became clear that managing
without budgets placed greater reliance on people-to-people and team-
to-team relationships and the clarity of the commitments (and conditions of satisfaction) they made to each other. Hiding behind budgets
and the plethora of excuses that they permit was no longer an option.
These cross-company commitments are now dynamic and react to
changes in the marketplace, so if an unanticipated and complex (but
large) customer requirement comes along, sales and production will discuss what should be done and how the current priority list should be
rescheduled. There is no budget to get in the way.

MANAGE CUSTOMER PROFITABILITY INFORMATION. In most companies, salespeople are recognized and rewarded on reaching sales targets, but when front-line people are making decisions concerning customer needs, it is essential that they have access to customer profitability information. Local staff at Handelsbanken are aware of customer profitability information. All processes have a standard cost that is attributed to the customer profit statement when an activity takes place. Moreover, *total customer profitability* is paramount. Thus, loss-leading products can sit alongside highly profitable ones within one customer account. Knowledge of customer profitability is indispensable when the solution is tailored for the customer. Many costs, such as packaging, distribution, marketing, training, credit, and management time, are seen as free services by salespeople, but in reality they are anything but free. Customization can easily result in losses unless the costs of customization are captured and taken into consideration in the customer profit statement.

Principle 6: Base Controls on Effective Governance and on a Range of Relative Performance Indicators

Most cases have switched their measurement emphasis from central control to multilevel *controls*. There is a world of difference between these two concepts. Central control means compliance with a fixed performance contract. Multilevel controls means knowing what's going on and only interfering when absolutely necessary. This means providing a multifaceted control system that includes effective governance from the center and that also supports local decision making. The information provided will normally include a wide range of key indicators and forecasts. Controls are strengthened because all those with an interest in the results *see the same information at the same time,* albeit at different levels of aggregation. Moreover, there are no middle managers filtering or spinning the information to make it look better than it is. As Gunnar Haglund at Ahlsell said, "There is only one truth." Such a management control system uses some or all of the following components: effective governance, fast financial actuals, trend analysis, rolling forecasts, key performance indicators, performance rankings, and management by exception.

USE EFFECTIVE GOVERNANCE. The corporate center has a range of risk management controls at its disposal. These include a governance framework that enables leaders to set boundaries and guidelines for strategy development and decision making. They then challenge managers to justify key assumptions and risks prior to making a major investment commitment. Only after such a robust challenge will both the center and business unit team be fully in accord.

Leaders also set reference levels for both medium-term aspirations and baseline performance expectations (for key indicators such as gross margins and return on capital). Thus leaders get the benefit of greater participation and commitment from front-line teams while retaining a sort of veto over high-risk strategies. They also have the ability to set minimum performance standards. Managers enjoy a high level of trust, but if it is abused then there is no court of appeal. People are allowed considerable tolerance if they make mistakes, but if they fail to live up to the principles and values expected of them, they will be shown the exit door pretty quickly. This emphasis on such values as integrity, openness, and fairness adds to the effectiveness of the risk management system.

PRODUCE FAST FINANCIAL ACTUALS. Actual financial results tend to be summarized and shown as trends and moving averages. They are also compared with prior periods. The analysis and presentation of financial information is fast and relevant. The objective is to have a real-time accounting system that is always up-to-date. Keeping accounting data to relevant (usually high-level) figures, together with the absence of budgets and variance analysis, lightens the reporting load.

USE TREND ANALYSIS. Some organizations, such as Borealis and Sight Savers, are using moving averages and twelve-month rolling views to replace the calendar-year focus on costs. Thus, the annual round of estimating and agreeing on cost requirements is eliminated. In its place is a continuous process of monitoring and (occasionally) implementing step-changes. These organizations believe this is a much more powerful way of maintaining the downward pressure on costs. Actuals might also be linked with rolling forecasts to show a continuous trend.

The U.K. charity Sight Savers International (SSI) uses a rolling twelve-month view. The latest month's results are added to the previous eleven months' actuals to give the results for the most recent rolling

TABLE 4 - 2

Sight Savers International's Internal Accounting Presentation

HISTORY—ACTUAL RESULTS

Account Heading	Previous Year Y⁻²	Last Year Y⁻¹	Current Year (Y⁰)		Latest Twelve Months
			Latest Month	Year-to-Date	

twelve-month period. By showing rolling twelve-month results, any seasonality, which might skew the results for the year to date, is removed. According to finance director Adrian Poffley, the impact of the latest decisions and activities can more easily be assessed using a trend of twelve months' results. Table 4-2 shows how SSI has adapted its internal (historic) reporting structure to meet the new performance management process.

USE ROLLING FORECASTS. All of our case examples use rolling forecasts in one form or another to provide a fast, high-level view of future performance. Thus, the forecasting process is "light touch" and fast (e.g., one day per quarter at Borealis). Because any changes will already have been circulated, there are rarely any surprises that concern senior managers. Without exception, rolling forecasts cover the important figures only. Orders, sales, costs, profits, and cash flows are the typical variables used. Moreover, these are "flash" forecasts that are often collated by "off-line" staff who have no interest in the implications of the figures. These forecasts perform a number of roles. They help senior executives to manage shareholder expectations, they enable finance people to consolidate and manage cash requirements, and they help operational managers to make decisions.

At some firms, rolling forecasts become the key trigger for action. The VP Finance at a global car manufacturer explains how his firm supports strategy reviews:

> Multiple interlocking cycles are the key to understanding our
> new management process. One-month "flash" forecasts look one
> quarter ahead; quarterly rolling forecasts look one year ahead;

annual rolling forecasts look four years ahead, and an annual strategic planning process looks ten years ahead. One forecast dovetails into another like cogs in a wheel. These forecasts form the core information for the monthly meetings, the development programs, and the strategy reviews. Managers build competence in sketching the future, and within that future lie the opportunities and threats that traditional budget-driven processes fail to see until it's too late.

USE KEY PERFORMANCE INDICATORS. KPIs provide two levers of control. One is based on monitoring performance against medium-term goals, and the other is based on monitoring performance within agreed-upon boundaries. With regard to progress against goals, KPIs tend to be high level and aimed at providing early warning signals that something might be going awry. They can be seen in historic terms (what actually happened, or *lagging indicators*) or in future terms (what is likely to happen, or *leading indicators*). They tend to be few in number and appropriate to the management level. When taken together, they provide a performance picture that tells managers what is happening now and likely to happen in the short-term future. With regard to their control functions, KPIs are usually based on ratios such as costs to income or costs and profits to capital.

KPIs have now become the primary control weapon at Sight Savers International. Adrian Poffley makes this point in his book *Financial Stewardship of Charities:*

> Key performance indicators must, between them, be sufficient and necessary to inform the charity's financial stewards about whether the financial performance and financial state of the charity are satisfactory or not. It is these KPIs that replace the target setting and control roles of budgets. Actual performance is expressed in terms of the KPIs, not in comparison to budget, and the KPIs guide the reader's judgment as to the satisfactoriness of the results. If well defined, the KPIs will reassure when all is well and raise a flag when corrective action is needed. Used as targets, the KPIs reflect the financial aspirations of the charity; as parameters they identify the boundaries within which performance is expected.[2]

SSI has begun to develop target ranges for its KPIs rather than precise outcomes, in recognition of the impossibility of forecasting with 100 percent accuracy. In effect this approach sets a minimum and maximum for each KPI. It is simply an extension of defining what is out of bounds, allowing the charity to acknowledge the imprecision of the exercise by saying "we want to see this indicator somewhere in this sort of range" without being overly prescriptive. SSI has accepted in principle that it might be necessary or desirable to change the KPI goal in light of actual circumstances. There is nothing sacrosanct about the KPIs, although changing them must not become a means of shifting the goalposts in order to dress up an unacceptable performance.

USE PERFORMANCE RANKINGS. In some cases, firms use internal per-formance-league tables. Both Handelsbanken and Ahlsell produce these monthly and make them immediately available for all managers to see. The tables inform managers about their relative performance and the extent to which they need to make further improvements.

MANAGE BY EXCEPTION. Managers, by and large, view performance by exception. At Handelsbanken, for example, senior managers are always looking for the exception or unusual patterns and trends that might reflect a change in customer behavior or branch performance. It is these changes that lead to a review of performance and a change of plan.

Changing Attitudes and Behaviors

We argued in chapter 1 that much of the dysfunctional behavior endemic to most organizations is determined by the annual budgeting process and its resultant fixed performance contract. Making a fixed promise that is subject to high levels of uncertainty and then requiring people to meet that promise at all costs is like putting the performance cart before the horse. The result is likely to be the distortion of prof-itability over time and, in exceptional circumstances, outright fraud.

The crucial point is that *it is the process that drives behavior, therefore to change behavior requires a different process.* This is not to say that be-cause there is an annual budget and fixed performance contract that undesirable behavior is an inevitable outcome. However, it does say that if the budgeting process and its resultant contract didn't exist then such behavior would be far less likely.

By removing the budgeting process and fixed performance contract, organizations can turn themselves into more virtuous organizations. Consider these ten statements that we believe reflect the behavior within many organizations that have abandoned the annual budgeting process and the fixed performance contract.

1. *"Always aim to improve upon and beat the competition."* Gone are all the games that people used to play. These were all geared toward meeting the agreed upon fixed target. Though they have some reasonably clear guidelines, people don't know the specific target in advance, so they must just keep doing their best to improve their position in the performance league table. It is the need to win rather than the need to survive that drives performance improvement.

2. *"Never let the team down and be the one that drains the profit-sharing pool."* Peer pressure is the most intense of all. Anyone who has been to a divisional meeting knowing that they are the one who has underperformed, causing everyone to suffer lower bonuses knows the feeling well. And they don't want it to happen again. Why is your performance inadequate? How can we help? These are typical responses in a "one-team" organization. While colleagues are helpful, you also know that if you don't improve, then you will not survive for long.

3. *"Always aim to know and care for customers."* The words "customer satisfaction" now begin to mean something. Most people are already aware that getting to know customers and taking care of their needs is much more likely to yield regular profits than engaging in high-pressure selling that might deliver a short-term result. Finding and keeping the right (profitable) customers supported with relevant information systems is the new approach.

4. *"Always share knowledge and resources with other teams—they are our partners!"* When profit pools are shared and rewards distributed fairly across the organization, it puts a whole new complexion on the issues of collaboration and sharing. Rather than fight-

ing each other for the favors of senior executives during the annual budgeting process, managers now share insights and best practices. The objective is that the performance of every team improves, thus raising the level of the profit-sharing pool.

5. *"Never acquire more resources than you need."* Spending what's in the budget doesn't make sense if there is no budget! The process of central allocation has gone away and been replaced by accountability against KPIs and an internal market within which resources can be acquired when needed (at an agreed upon price). Of course large projects still need to be professionally prepared, presented, and approved, but this can be done at any time—it doesn't depend on the annual budgeting process when everyone is jockeying for position.

6. *"Always aim to challenge (and reduce) costs."* As business units are now measured on a few key indicators (including profit), everyone wants to eliminate any costs that don't add value. Ultimately they know that this supports their employment prospects, as having the lowest costs not only improves their position in the league table, but it also makes the whole organization more competitive, and thus more durable.

7. *"Always have the ability to understand root causes."* The budgeting system was all about explaining why the predetermined plan was not working. Now there is no fixed plan, so you have to explain why competitors operating in the same market as you are producing better results. Thus you need to look beneath the numbers at the root causes of problems. It is this type of analysis that leads to real learning and improvement.

8. *"Always 'tell it like it is' and share bad news."* Because people were being measured against some fixed number, any significant variations from the plan (good or bad) were treated with special care. If it was good news then the effects would be held back (to compensate for bad news), and if it was bad news, then the reverse would happen. Now there is a culture of openness and sharing. Information reaches many different people at the same time. And there are few controllers who want to massage the figures. So sharing bad news is seen as a sign of strength rather than weakness.

9. *"Always do your best, never fudge the numbers."* Fudging the numbers was all about meeting the agreed target. Now that this target has been removed, the need for creative accounting has gone. Not only does it save a lot of time, but it also reduces stress as people no longer need to put their professional ethics on the line.

10. *"Always challenge conventional wisdom."* In a culture of continuous improvement, little progress will be made if people do not challenge the way things are done. People at every level are now open and prepared to listen to new ideas. But with so much baggage remaining from the budgeting system there is still much to be done!

Chapter Summary

- The best practices from the cases we have examined suggest there are six key principles that organizations should adhere to if they wish to manage without annual budgets:
  1. Base goals on external benchmarks rather than on internally negotiated targets.
  2. Base evaluation and rewards on relative improvement contracts with hindsight rather than on fixed performance contracts agreed upon in advance.
  3. Make action planning a continuous and inclusive process rather than an annual and restrictive exercise.
  4. Make resources available as required under KPI accountability rather than allocated in advance on the basis of annual budgets.
  5. Coordinate cross-company actions dynamically according to prevailing customer demand rather than a predetermined annual master budget.
  6. Base controls on effective governance and on a range of relative performance indicators rather than on fixed reviews against annual plans and budgets.
- By removing the budgeting process and fixed performance contract, firms are able to change the attitudes and behaviors of people at every level of the organization. In particular, they are likely to eradicate the undesirable behaviors that result from setting a fixed target that must be met even though the outcome is highly uncertain.

Chapter Five

Insights into Implementation

> Culture changes only after you have altered people's actions, after the
> new behavior produces some group benefit for a period of time, and
> after people see the connection between the new actions and the
> performance improvement.[1]
> —JOHN KOTTER

Little uniformity exists in how firms have approached the implementation of beyond budgeting. Though some have used consultants to help with process design, few so far have used them to aid with the abandonment of the budgeting process and the implementation of its replacement. However, after interviewing more than one hundred managers at all levels and consistently asking what went well and what went not so well, we have gathered some guidelines to help prospective users.

- *Defining the case for change and an outline vision:* It's an essential first step.
- *Convincing the board:* Be prepared.
- *Getting started:* It's easier than you think.
- *Designing the model and implementing new processes:* It's coherence that matters.
- *Training and educating people:* It's never enough.
- *Rethinking the role of finance:* It's an opportunity to add value.

- *Changing behavior:* It's driven by new processes, not by management decree.
- *Evaluating the benefits:* There are plenty of quick wins.
- *Consolidating the gains:* It's about winning hearts and minds at the top.

Defining the Case for Change and an Outline Vision: It's an Essential First Step

Implementing beyond budgeting, whatever the initial scope of the changes envisioned, is a significant change program and needs to be handled accordingly. It is not just about changing a process and putting in an alternative process or set of processes. It is about changing mind-sets and achieving a different coherence in the way the organization as a whole is managed. The starting point should therefore be to define the case for change and an outline vision. Without this the project leader cannot expect to win the necessary commitment at the top and subsequently build a groundswell of support for the change throughout the organization. The case for change should be both a clear statement of the "current pain" experienced with the budget based model, as well as the benefits to be gained by adopting the new vision.

Most people see the first beyond budgeting opportunity in terms of switching to a more adaptive performance management process. Others see it in terms of a new management philosophy designed to sweep away bureaucracy and the centralized mind-set that supports it. Given the range of these perspectives, it is evident that the vision and scope of the project must be made clear from the outset.

This doesn't mean that it needs to have defined limits (many projects designed to change processes have gone on to embrace cultural change). But it does mean that the initial road map must be made clear and that participants must know and share its direction and objectives.

How the proposed changes will be implemented is another important part of defining the scope. For example, some companies might choose to make changes across the whole group simultaneously, some might choose to start with the head office–to–business unit link, and others might choose one complete unit or division and try it out. These are important and far from straightforward considerations. Resources, cost, time, and risk are all factors that must be considered before project leaders decide on the final scope of their proposals. One thing, however, is certain: Changes that affect management behavior and rewards cannot be half-hearted. Nor can those managers affected be accountable to people working within different management styles and systems. Unless those people engaged in the process believe it is "forever," they are unlikely to give their total commitment, and the project will probably end in failure. If a pilot program is the chosen way forward, then at the very least it should involve a complete business entity, such as an independent business unit or division.

Although some leaders see the replacement of the budgeting process as a finance initiative, this can be a mistake. Of course, finance has significant involvement, but to succeed, the project team needs input from a broad cross-functional team that includes representatives from human resources, IT, strategy, change management, and, most important of all, operations. This team should lend credence to the project and help to convince others across the organization of its merits.

How a Pilot Program Failed to Lead
to Full Change at a Large U.K. Company

Failing to agree upon a shared vision for the project and focusing too much on the finance changes can cause the project to undershoot its potential. This was one of the lessons learned by a large U.K. company. Its change director explains:

> Managing without budgets in a large company like ours is a real challenge. What we decided to do was to pilot the program in one of our divisions. The pilot exceeded our expectations, but embedding the principles underlying the pilot across the rest of the organization has taken longer than originally envisaged. We held a number of workshops to map our strategy process and to determine what inputs, resources, controls, and outputs were required at each step. The reaction from operating managers and internal customers was very enthusiastic. "One of the best initiatives ever to come out of finance," was a typical reaction. Having said that, it was senior managers who drove the project. Engaging people in the thinking

and planning behind the new KPIs was instrumental in gaining complete "buy in" to the new approach. It became a cultural revolution. The result is that everyone is part of the strategy process and we don't have to wait until the end of the year to evaluate our progress. Operating people are quick to tell us if our strategy is not working.

But the initial enthusiasm began to wane when other priorities including large-scale mergers absorbed the attention of head office sponsors. Nevertheless most of the principles within the pilot are now in place in many businesses across the organization. It has been a real eye-opener and has demonstrated to everyone what we can do if we are given more scope to use our knowledge and experience. It also shows how quickly people can learn about the business if they are given the accountability for results.

Convincing the Board: Be Prepared

Convincing members of the board that managing without budgets will bring significant benefits without too many downsides is a key role for the project team. Sometimes this is not much of a problem if the project champion is already an important member of the board (this was the case in the majority of the companies we studied). The board will naturally be concerned about the impact on internal control and the effects on the perceptions of analysts and bankers.

There are two key issues. One is whether the company is maintaining effective corporate governance and internal controls. The other is whether the proposed changes will affect the company's ability to forecast future earnings and, perhaps most important of all, avoid the need to upset the market with unpleasant surprises. Neither issue should be a difficult challenge. Those companies that have done away with budgets have found that the new information system is faster, more open, and offers better controls. The issue of forecasting is even less of a problem. Indeed, the problem *with budgeting* is that few companies have the ability to see ahead. Those firms that have eliminated budgets have, without exception, moved to a system of rolling forecasts that invariably cover the next fiscal year-end thus placing the CEO in a much stronger position to anticipate financial results. They have also introduced leading

KPIs that help them to anticipate change. Borealis provides an example of how to approach the board with a rational case for replacing budgeting, as discussed in the next section.

Convincing the Board at Borealis

When Bjarte Bogsnes and his team were in the early stages of planning the introduction of adaptive processes at Borealis, they were confronted many times with the questions "How do we control the business without budgets?" and "Why take the risk?" Over a period of several months, the board demanded answers to these questions, as well as asking for details of how the alternative model would work and what benefits would be gained from adopting it. Bogsnes made the case for change through a series of presentations and discussions with the board. Though the case was well prepared and presented, there was little formality. A brief presentation to the board was followed by a discussion about risks and benefits (but not costs).

Two primary risks were considered: that costs would explode because of fewer controls, and that decision making would be paralyzed. Both were thought to be so minimal that they were not taken too seriously. Line managers needed even less convincing than the board. They knew that the cyclical nature of the business severely diminished the value of most annual budgets and therefore were more than happy to embrace some new ideas, especially ones that gave them more flexibility to deal with opportunities and problems as they arose.

The fact that senior management was prepared to sanction the dismantling of the budgeting process sent an important message to all the company's managers—namely, that senior management was prepared to tackle sacred cows and deal with issues that had gone unchallenged for years. This created a new atmosphere that has since prepared the company for continuous change. Bogsnes addressed the question of risk in the following way:

> We have good, capable people who take their jobs seriously. They
> know what to do. The likelihood of chaos is minimal. We should
> also consider the risks of not doing it. What would happen? We
> would carry on as normal with no one challenging costs and

> everyone demanding more resources than the company can afford. Competitiveness would continue to decline. Now let me turn to the question of control. How much control do we have now? Approving and following up detailed budgets creates a perceived feeling of control and power, but too often blurs the real issues instead. But if it should fail, budgets can be reintroduced overnight. There is no need to burn the manuals the first year, and the organization will certainly not have forgotten how to budget.... There might be some lost face, but that is nothing compared to the upside potential.

Bogsnes did not have a problem convincing senior managers that changes were necessary. However, convincing everyone that there was a viable alternative proved to be a much greater challenge.

> The breakthrough came when we realized that the only way to face this challenge was to break the budget down into its purposes and demonstrate how each would be achieved within the new system. We spent a considerable amount of time designing scorecards, cost reports, and activity-based accounting models that—taken together—provided a coherent (and convincing) approach. Only when we were confident that we had 80 percent of the picture did we proceed toward implementation.

Table 5-1 shows how Bogsnes made his presentation to the board. It depicts how each function of budgeting is executed in a different, but no less comprehensive, way.

Getting Started: It's Easier Than You Think

As we noted earlier in this chapter, abandoning budgeting usually needs a vision statement describing how it is going to work and what supporting systems will be needed. But of equal importance, it should be sold and implemented (as indeed it was in many of the organizations we have reported on) on the basis of what it isn't rather than what it is. In other words, the work that is eliminated becomes a major, if not the primary attraction. Less work (an unusual feature of a change program!) is an easy sell to many operating people already overburdened with administrative chores and unnecessary meetings. This was the approach taken at Rhodia.

TABLE 5 - 1

Replacing the Budgeting Processes at Borealis

The Budget Was Used for:	We Achieve the Same Through:
Setting targets	Medium-term relative targets (benchmarks if step-changes required)
	Key performance indicators aligned with goals
Improvement initiatives	Actions derived from strategy reviews
Prioritizing and allocating investment/projects resources	Small projects—local approval (trend reporting)
	Medium projects—local/central approval (varying hurdle rates)
	Major projects—central approval (case by case)
Coordinating plans and actions	Process linkages (through IT system)
	Service level agreements between central services and operating units
Controlling fixed costs	Trend reporting and moving averages
	Benchmarking
Controlling performance	Fast actuals compared with prior period
	Rolling forecasts (e.g., 5 quarters in advance)
	KPIs relative to last year, competition, etc. (Including league tables)
	Trends
Delegating authority	Devolving authority to meet KPIs to operating teams

Getting Started at Rhodia

At a cocktail meeting in April 1999, Rhodia chairman Jean-Pierre Tirouflet announced that he wanted to abandon the central planning and budgeting process. "You have one month to propose an alternative approach" was his ultimatum to the finance director. The concepts were discussed and confirmed with external consultants in June and presented to a meeting of the group's top forty managers in July 1999. In August a decision was made to go ahead. Jacky Pinçon was appointed as the manager of the "Spring" project (as it became known) and has led the project since that time. Apart from the cost savings from not spending half of each year budgeting, the objectives were to build a faster-responding organization; to align strategies, plans, and forecasts; to decentralize operations; and to develop a more dynamic corporate culture.

A new planning methodology was designed and presented to business unit management teams across the company. The budgeting process was simultaneously dismantled. Operating businesses were given no choice: From that point on, there would be no other performance management process in place. In the rollout phase, however, the levels of competence and the ability to operate with the new methodology were mixed. This led to a regimented approach from the center. In other words, enterprises and business units had to comply with templates and time scales that enabled group executives to demand strategies and actions according to a program that provided the group with the information it needed.

Training manuals and strategy and planning templates were designed, which helped Pinçon to roll out the new system across the group's 150 sites. There was no pilot program. The decision was to go for it and make the new system operative immediately, with no budget being prepared for the year 2000. The other key approach to implementation was not to introduce Spring as another major change program. The organization was already suffering from "change fatigue." Therefore, there were no major conferences. In fact, there was very little fanfare at all. Operating people didn't need much persuading. They just needed some help.

Though different parts of the organization have progressed at different speeds, with the direct support of the president, Spring has blossomed. Pinçon has spent most of his time training managers and making many follow-up visits to carry out competence audits. However, with limited resources, there is only so much education and hand-holding that can be done. As Pinçon noted at the time, "The year 2000 was about understanding the strategy process, 2001 is about action planning, and it will be 2002 before managers gain a real understanding of the forecasting process."

Designing the Model and Implementing New Processes: It's Coherence That Matters

The annual budgeting process connects every part of an organization and influences how people think and behave at every level. Any changes must therefore take account of these effects. This means, for example, that change cannot just be about implementing stretch targets or rolling forecasts without realigning recognition and rewards and reestablishing coherence in the whole process. Two experiences of how *not* to abandon budgeting illustrate the problems that come with a lack of coherence. The first concerns a large consumer products group and the second concerns a large telecommunications company in the late 1990s.

How a Lack of Coherence Undermined Attempts to Replace the Traditional Budgeting Process at a Large Consumer Products Group

After abandoning the budgeting process for 1998–1999 the company introduced "stretch forecasts" and told its managers to set their goals at more ambitious levels than they would have done under the old budgeting system (thus overcoming the propensity to agree on incremental targets), and that they would not be held accountable if they got them wrong. So managers, taking the chairman at his word, estimated revenues and resource requirements at a much higher level (pleasing their bosses); but their pleasure turned to dismay as these forecasts turned out to be hugely inflated, causing costs and inventories to increase and ending in huge write-offs. The result was serious damage to the company's reputation with suppliers, customers, and shareholders.

The problem was that, though claiming it had replaced the budgeting process, the company had failed to replace the plan-make-and-sell business model on which it was based. In other words, the implementation of stretch forecasts manifested itself in aspirational estimates of likely sales rather than those estimates being derived from a well-grounded strategy and action planning process. In particular, they did not have reliable rolling forecasts that were built from the bottom up on the anticipated needs of real customers. They were, in effect, just numbers on spreadsheets that reflected what senior managers wanted to see. Moreover, salespeople, if they are rewarded on volumes, have little or no interest in *net margins*, but they do have an interest in ensuring that products are available for sale. It was perhaps a case of empowerment without accountability—a fatal mixture, and guaranteed to fail.

How a Lack of Coherence Undermined Attempts
to Replace the Traditional Budgeting Process at a
Large Telecommunications Company

Recent success in the data communications and mobile markets had led to a group with diverse businesses subject to varying degrees of competition and change. Because the management processes were developed for the local telephone business, they were less suited to the faster-moving businesses of data and wireless. This, together with a finance benchmarking study that showed the company's systems to be in the lowest quartile, suggested to the finance team that they should shake up their planning and budgeting processes and look for better ways of managing that part of the business.

A number of issues militated against a successful implementation. First, the scope of the project was to improve the performance of the finance department as measured by the benchmarking study that looked at best practices and cost. Such a limited approach places immediate restrictions on how far the changes can go. As project leaders discovered, unless many other related issues such as abandonment of the fixed performance contract (and especially the realignment of rewards) are also covered, the chances of success are greatly diminished.

Second, the finance department cannot drive through such changes on its own. Such a project requires a multifunctional team to deal with the various management changes needed. Furthermore, the solutions developed were one size fits all and did not take into account the significant differences between business units, such as the fast moving, mobile telephones business and the slower moving, local telephone network services.

Third, there appeared to be a reluctance to devolve meaningful decision-making responsibility to operating managers. Fear of losing control was the likely factor, but there was also a concern that line management would not be willing to accept more accountability.

And fourth (and perhaps most important), there was a pervasive belief that managers are driven by annual incentives linked to a fixed performance contract based on the budget. Thus, any attempt to change the budgeting cycle would inevitably lead to changes in the way that incentives and bonuses were agreed upon and paid, which, in turn, would lead to uncertainty surrounding the final compensation package.

The primary lesson from this case is that if a company tries to make fundamental changes to core management processes such as budgeting, then it cannot avoid facing a number of issues such as recognition and rewards. (That is, it must deal with the issues surrounding the performance contract.) Unless these are aligned, and coherence reestablished with the changes being made, there is little chance of sustained progress. Nevertheless, the company's attempts to move away from the budgeting model were not without success. More emphasis on understanding cost drivers and better forecasting processes were among its notable achievements.

Training and Educating People: It's Never Enough

If there was anything that most project leaders regretted with hindsight, it was not spending more time and effort on training and education. Combining well-designed systems and a rollout program with excellent training materials has enabled project leaders to make real progress at Rhodia. However, they were careful not to create "head office experts" who could be called upon to support operating people. Project leaders made it clear that it was everyone's responsibility to become familiar with the new processes as quickly as possible. The task was as much about understanding the business as about implementing a new process. Time was devoted to designing comprehensive training materials in the form of written manuals and self-learning materials on CD-ROM.

Swedish wholesaler Ahlsell has another reason for offering comprehensive training programs. It uses adaptive processes as a key element in improving the performance of acquired companies, and therefore has probably spent more time on this issue than other firms.

Training and Educating People at Ahlsell

Ahlsell recognized that managing without budgets required the company to build up the capabilities of its people. Accordingly, employees now receive training in the company's way of working and in leadership skills through the "Ahlsell College." Every new recruit receives an initial two days of training at the training center (located at the central warehouse), with courses being held every two months in groups of thirty to thirty-five people. Other courses are also offered. Any training to improve competencies is seen as a value-adding process and is available as required, but the cost is charged to units.

The head office finance department educates everyone in how to read a profit and loss account and in what actions are required to improve performance. The department has developed simple handbooks to help front-line people understand and operate the systems. Any instructions (e.g., how to use the information systems within units) are clearly labeled "For your help" on the cover. These guides are not seen as rules and procedures but as an efficient way to help units. The onus is on individuals to get themselves up to speed. As a result, front-line managers have now become the "controllers" of their own self-managed teams. Ahlsell also encourages people to meet with others to foster learning. In addition, they have a few "traveling controllers" to support front-line people.

Rethinking the Role of Finance: It's an Opportunity to Add Value

The success of managing without budgets will be fleeting unless the role played by the finance team is realigned with the new processes. Indeed, a few of our cases indicated that this was a step that was done poorly and was regretted later. This is a time of maximum uncertainty for the finance team, and they need to know exactly where they stand. Those firms that have done this effectively have involved the finance people in all the detailed proposals, explained how their roles will change, and ensured they have the training to meet the challenges ahead. At Bulmers the benefits to the finance team were palpable, with a reduction in the workload and the stress that went with it. And at Swedish ball-bearing manufacturer SKF, the perception of finance people was noticeably different after implementing the new processes.

Creating More Time for Value-Adding Work at Bulmers

After the shock of hearing how few front-line people valued their work, the finance team at Bulmers was determined to make sweeping changes. These were not only profound for operating people but also for the finance team itself.

In the first year of managing without budgets, there was no overtime work (fourteen-hour days were previously common), not only saving tens of thousands of dollars but also alleviating considerable stress from such an intense work schedule. During the same year, the management team also implemented a reorganization of the business (a task that previously would have entailed multiple budget recompilations), a new target-setting and KPI-based reporting system, and a new accounting system that reduced the monthly closing period from eight to four days, and completed the year-end accounts. All this work was done with no extra staff and no overtime.

Enhancing the Perception of Finance People at SKF

In most large organizations, if local managers receive telephone calls or e-mail from group finance people, it is rarely good news. It is more likely to involve a report or explanation that has not yet been forthcoming, or a request to attend a meeting to discuss financial progress. The perception that operating managers have of their financial colleagues is one of "head office controllers" rather than internal consultants. This was the case at SKF, but it changed significantly when the budgeting process was abandoned in 1995.

Anders Forsberg, group financial controller at the time, explains the impact:

> Once you break away from the constraints of budgeting you begin to focus on the more important questions. We now support operating managers by helping them to answer questions about which parts of the business (including product lines, customer segments, individual customers, and processes) are creating value and which aren't. Should we outsource underperforming processes? Should we enter or exit certain market segments? Should we increase customer satisfaction? The outcome[s] of these and many other alternative decisions are tested within the new forecasting model, and decisions taken that maximize business value. We also keep a sharp eye on competitive performance either using an internal or external league table of benchmark businesses (or a combination of both). Strategies and plans continuously unfold as new knowledge

emerges. There were other unexpected surprises. For example, the reputation of the finance team grew in stature. While we were previously seen as controllers and bean counters, we are now seen as real business partners providing a value-added service. It gives you a better feeling about your worth inside the organization.

Changing Behavior: It's Driven by New Processes, Not by Management Decree

The idea that behavior change follows process change is supported by most of our cases. And, once again, the key driver is what is no longer done (managing through annual budgets) rather than what is now done (managing without annual budgets). The key point is that managers don't need to be told what to do: It soon becomes obvious that with no detailed budget to define their targets and dictate their actions, they have no choice but to accept greater responsibility for their actions and more accountability for their results.

Behavioral changes are, of course, hard to pin down and support with hard evidence. But one key observable change is the acceptance of greater performance responsibility by business units. With no detailed budget to specify the performance contract between superiors and subordinates, there is, by default, much more scope for subordinates to achieve results, provided they clearly understand how their performance will be evaluated and rewarded. This simple transfer of responsibility has a powerful galvanizing effect on management behavior. We can see these effects at Bulmers. But we have also visited a company that thought it was decentralized and that performance responsibility was devolved to local businesses, when in reality the budget still ruled and remained an insurmountable wall. We start with this example.

How the Failure to Change Existing Budgeting Processes Led to the Ineffective Decentralization of a U.K. Building Services Company

The company was the largest U.K. subsidiary of a global giant that had over the past decade gained a reputation for being a successful exemplar of a modern decentralized organization. Its chairman had been interviewed by the *Harvard Business Review* and became a media star. He believed that the only way to structure a complex global organization was to decentralize responsibilities and make the organization as simple and local as possible. He stated that the company's managers had well-defined sets of responsibilities, clear accountability, and maximum degrees of freedom to execute actions.

Our visit to the company was organized in such a way that we were able to discuss these issues with senior finance and human resources executives, and some operating managers from regional and local depots. The extent of disagreement about how they managed the business caught us by surprise. While the group finance people clearly thought that local leaders had adequate freedom and capabilty to manage the business effectively, local managers took an opposite view. A couple of examples will illustrate these divisions.

The building and contracting industry in the United Kingdom is not known for its ability to provide innovative solutions to its customers. It's a mature market with heavy emphasis on price. We asked, "Is there a paucity of ideas and radical thinking at the company?" "Not at all," was the reply from both a regional and a profit center manager. They elaborated: "It would take us just two days to come up with a dozen radical ideas, but if we couldn't demonstrate that they would bring immediate profits, then we wouldn't be given a hearing." "There are no simple routes for the development and communication of new ideas," was another comment we heard. Such views came as a surprise to head office executives who believed they were open and responsive to new ideas. The budgeting and control system militates against such processes being effective in practice.

Another example concerned the opportunity to acquire a star salesman who became available rather inconveniently during the middle of the year (i.e., not when the budget was being submitted). Everything about him was right, including his experience, his knowledge of customers and competition, and his ideas, which might have helped the company gain access to new markets. However, the local manager was over his budgeted headcount, and despite remonstrations up the line, he couldn't get approval to take on anyone else. So he turned to one of his colleagues in another profit center. Could the salesman be accommodated within his budget? The answer was no. Why should he take the risk when the same opportunity might happen to him next week? Such is the perversity of the budgeting process that a person who could add significantly to the company's intangible assets and potential profitability was allowed to join the competition. This is a story from the front line at the company. Given that one of its key value drivers was the capability of its people, this is a sad reflection on its ability to make the most of these supposedly highly valued assets.

Although the company is a separate legal entity and its managers have full responsibility and accountability for its profit and loss account and balance sheet, the authority to respond quickly to market opportunities and competitive threats was heavily constrained by the group's reporting and control systems. Moreover, there was evidence of the "silo" mentality. Few of its profit centers cooperated with each other. It was evident that they had little confidence and trust that any such help and support would be reciprocated, suspecting that it might even be used by another business unit to gain a temporary advantage. The profit center manager's task was not an easy one. For a start, such managers carry a huge burden of central overheads, in some cases up to 50 percent of their costs. These overheads were, by and large, allocated by sales, so if the sales increased but margins were low, a ludicrous situation could arise whereby profits fell.

The meeting was a revelation for all concerned. It was obvious that the perceptions of decentralized decision making were quite different from the perspectives of group leaders, business unit leaders, and frontline managers.

How New Processes Led to a Change in Behavior at Bulmers

Bulmers is a 115-year-old maker of hard cider based in rural England. The annual budget contract spelled out to all managers just what they had to deliver in the year ahead. Negotiating the numbers soaked up most of the energy of operating managers during the annual budgeting round, and thereafter they were well versed in explaining what went wrong. Abandoning this process and cutting the umbilical cord of dependency was thus a severe shock to the management system. Lesley

Jackson (finance director of the U.K. subsidiary at the time) recounts what happened:

> Our first experience of managing without budgets was a real eye-opener. All we said to the sales, marketing, and production teams was that we wanted them to improve their profit contributions by a percentage they clearly thought was ridiculous. We knew there was no way they could get there by doing business as usual. They had to think and act differently. They found it really hard. In some cases it nearly led to nervous breakdowns. Some people came back and demanded budgets. They clearly found it much easier to produce a set of numbers than action plans that depended on many variables. At first the factory team were puzzled as to how they would know what to produce in month five, six, or seven, even though they agreed that we wouldn't know until a few weeks in advance what customers would demand. So we agreed to move to a twelve-week rolling production plan.
>
> This was just one of many changes we made as we worked our way through the new process. The other idea we had was to ban spreadsheets. We didn't want detailed numbers. We just wanted a few presentation slides and a convincing case. We asked them time and again: How will you deliver? In some cases we gave them financial help. Eventually they all responded with positive proposals. But what was really important was that they really believed in them. In one step we had moved from nebulous numbers on the budget statement to key performance indicators on bulletin boards in the factory and sales offices.

Evaluating the Benefits: There Are Plenty of Quick Wins

Demonstrating short-term wins is important to keep the resistors at bay. There will always be people looking for the first signs of failure, so there is nothing better than to show them hard evidence of success. Short-term wins should have three characteristics: They should be visible (people can see the results for themselves), they should be unambiguous, and they should be clearly related to the changes. Whereas the "big wins" come from behavioral changes (and are difficult to relate to specific financial results), there are some benefits that can appear relatively quickly. Here are a few:

- *The cost savings from not budgeting.* One immediate benefit is a reduction in the time and cost spent on budgeting and reporting. For example, Borealis measured the time spent on budgeting and compared it with the time now spent on forecasting, which showed a dramatic reduction. The cost savings from not producing (often irrelevant) management reports was one of the surprises at Bulmers. One example concerned a production manager who maintained his own detailed reports that evidently provided little strategic value yet cost a huge sum to produce! The payback on the changes—both tangible and intangible—has therefore been quickly in evidence. Volvo Cars is another company that estimated that its previous planning, budgeting, and control processes absorbed around 20 percent of total management time. By abandoning these processes and managing in a different way, managers have saved significant wasted effort and gained more time to focus on strategy, action planning, and beating the competition.
- *The cost savings from reducing bureaucracy and changing behavior.* A key element in the Borealis approach was to achieve a low cost base. It adopted a three-pronged approach. First, it restructured the business. Second, it adopted trend analysis to manage fixed costs and eradicate the "protect the budget" mentality. And third, it introduced activity-based management to better understand the causes of costs and thus be in a stronger position to challenge them. The company has succeeded in reducing costs by 30 percent within the first five years of managing without budgets.
- *Faster response from more adaptive processes.* Making strategy an open, continuous, and adaptive process is perhaps the key benefit gained by firms that operate in a fast-changing environment. Regular rolling forecasts can be helpful in this regard, and access to resources when they are needed can be critical. Underlying these approaches is the shredding of the bureaucracy that still plagues most large organizations.

This is exactly what happened at Bulmers. Management accountant David Berkeley made this observation:

> We removed the barriers that prevented fast communication, including much of the command and control structure that has run this company for years. We tackled the stifling bureaucracy, along with the central planning apparatus, staff empires, "memos from head office," "special studies," and other classic features of how large companies work as decisions grind their way through the system. "If it's to be it's up to me" sums up our new approach to management. People now communicate in a different way—saying what they mean rather than couching their views in the shady language of corporate politics. Speaking directly to people across traditional boundaries without going up and down the official organizational channels doesn't sound very revolutionary, but it has made an enormous difference to how quickly and effectively things get done inside our business.

Consolidating the Gains: It's about Winning Hearts and Minds at the Top

In a number of cases, significant progress has been made toward embedding the principles of adaptive processes only for a new CEO or the board of an acquiring company to undo many of the gains. The experience of a large U.S. retail food group after it was acquired by a large European multinational reinforces the point that it is essential that the adoption of beyond budgeting principles is supported by the executive board and recognized to be a key competitive advantage. Better still, it should play a key role in the decentralization of performance responsibility inside the organization. These issues will be dealt with more fully in part 2 of this book.

How the Return of Budgeting and Its Associated Bureaucracy Affected Morale after a Large U.S. Company Was Sold

A U.S. retail food group had a history of 20 percent growth in sales and profits for the previous ten years. Through this period it had managed without a traditional budgeting process. The chairman did not believe in budgets because he thought they restricted flexibility. Goals were set relative to prior years,' and daily profit and loss accounts told managers whether further action was necessary. Overheads were monitored and managed using a KPI relative to sales. However, managers would try to protect the level of marketing expenditure as this was critical to long-term success. According to a finance manager, "it was a simple structure. There was a lot of transparency."

Since the takeover of the group by a large European company the budgeting processes have returned and the culture has changed markedly. One of the finance managers made these comments:

> The budget for 2001 started in April and was pushed into departments and broken down into months. There is now little ownership. Previously, when the company was owned by the directors there was not much hierarchy. Now "big brother" is kind of watching. When the business is growing at 20 percent there isn't a problem. My fear is that when this growth slows down we will have people from head office telling us to cut here or cut there.

One of the senior executives made this telling observation:

> In a large public company when you identify a potential loss of say $2 million you spread it over four quarters rather than take it as it comes. Why is it so important to play games when you know the truth? Public companies are judged on how well you meet your numbers. So everyone puts in contingencies to cover themselves in case the outcome is worse than they expect. In large public companies people focus on managing their careers rather than the business. We focused on managing the brand. That's the biggest difference. We were emotionally connected. They are not.

A number of lessons can be learned from the way that firms have approached implementation:

- Making a clear case for change is the first step. It should be based on both "the current pain" and the benefits envisioned and be used to build a groundswell of support for moving forward.
- Some issues that need careful consideration are deciding whether the scope of the project should be restricted to process improvement and whether the changes should be tried out in a pilot site.
- Convincing members of the board that managing without budgets will bring significant benefits without too many adverse side effects is a key role for the project team. Boards are particularly concerned about the perception that analysts, bankers, and non-executives will have concerning a weakening of controls. Board members are more likely to support the project if they are convinced that these are not major hurdles.
- Abandoning budgeting can be sold and implemented on the basis of what it *isn't* as well as what it is. In other words, the work that is eliminated is one of the significant benefits, and less work is an easy sell to many operating people already overburdened with administrative chores and unnecessary meetings.
- The traditional budgeting process (for all its flaws) represents a coherent model, so any changes must also be coherent. This means, for example, that the process cannot just be about implementing stretch targets or rolling forecasts without realigning recognition and rewards.
- If there is anything that most project leaders regret, it is not spending more time and effort on training and education. Combining well-designed systems with a rollout program supported by excellent training materials has enabled project leaders to make real progress. However, they were careful not to create

"head office experts" who could be called upon to support operating people.

- The success of managing without budgets will be short-lived unless the role played by the finance team is realigned with the new processes. This is a time of maximum uncertainty for the finance group, and they need to know, in advance, exactly where they stand. Those firms that have managed this effectively have involved the finance people in all the detailed changes and ensured they have the training to meet the challenges ahead.
- The recognition that behavior change follows process change is supported by most of our cases. The key point is that managers don't need to be told what to do: It soon becomes obvious that with no detailed budget to define their targets and dictate their actions, they have no choice but to accept greater responsibility for their actions and more accountability for their results.
- Demonstrating short-term wins is important to keep the resistors at bay. There will always be people looking for the first signs of failure, so there is nothing better than to show them hard evidence of success. Cost savings are one example. They are usually evident (and measurable) within months.
- Consolidating the gains ultimately depends on the new adaptive processes changing attitudes and behaviors at the highest level in the corporate center. Even then it is vulnerable to a new CEO who has a different set of beliefs. That is why choosing successive executive leaders who believe in the power of the beyond budgeting culture is so important.

Part III

The Radical Decentralization Opportunity: Enabling Leaders to Create a High Performance Organization

Chapter Six

How Three Organizations Removed the Barriers to Change

Self-managed teams are far more productive than any other form of organizing. There is a clear correlation between participation and productivity; in fact, productivity gains in truly self-managed work environments are at minimum 35 percent higher than in traditionally managed organizations.[1]
—MARGARET WHEATLEY

A number of organizations have seen the opportunity of abandoning budgeting not just in terms of improving processes, but also in terms of radically decentralizing their organizations. In this context, their leaders have taken the view that budgeting is the defining process that perpetuates their cultural norms. Thus, only by removing it will the way be clear to make the kind of changes necessary to fundamentally change behavior. And the key behavioral feature they want to encourage is the acceptance of performance responsibility by front-line people. Some people use the term *decentralization* to describe this idea. Others use *devolution, self-governance,* or *empowerment.* Whichever expression is used, the intent is to transfer the responsibility for strategic thinking and decision making from the center to people closer to the customer. The extent and speed of this change depend on the type of business and the maturity and experience of front-line managers.

Leaders in these organizations are saying that if people are given the responsibility and scope to perform and if they have clear goals, a framework of values, and information that they can rely on, then they will be self-motivated to improve their performance. Such individuals will also behave in the interests of the team and the organization and will support their value systems, pursue quality outcomes, focus on satisfying internal and external customers, and operate within ethical boundaries. Although managers need some operating guidelines (e.g., a baseline cost-to-income ratio) and different ways of evaluating performance (including relative performance measures), *they don't need detailed budgets.*

This chapter features three cases that have used the devolution of responsibility as their central management philosophy.

- Ahlsell is a Swedish wholesaler with sales of around $1 billion.
- Leyland Trucks is a U.K. truck manufacturer (now part of the U.S.-based PACCAR group).
- Svenska Handelsbanken is our most mature case. It is therefore no surprise that it should appear in both the "adaptive process" and "decentralization" parts of this book.

In the same way that we dealt with the "process" cases in part II, we will examine the three "decentralization" cases using three chapters. This chapter describes what our featured cases have done. Chapter 7 extracts some principles and best practices, and chapter 8 examines how leaders have risen to the key challenge of changing the centralized mind-set.

Ahlsell

Ahlsell is a long-established Swedish wholesaler of plumbing and heating products. In recent times it has added tools and electrical, do-it-yourself, and refrigeration products to its portfolio. The recession of the early 1990s provided the catalyst for more radical thinking, and, after witnessing the success at Handelsbanken, Ahlsell's directors decided to abandon its central bureaucracy and empower its front-line people. The first priority was to expand the number of profit centers from 14 to 160 (after more recent acquisitions, there are now around 200).

Gunnar Haglund, finance director, is the architect of the new management model. He led its implementation in 1995 and has subsequently developed it further. Since 1996 Ahlsell has acquired sixteen companies, which account in a static market for 90 percent of its revenue growth over the past six years. Since abandoning budgeting, Ahlsell has been steadily extracting advantages. These are now reflected in more satisfied and highly skilled employees, improved customer satisfaction, and superior financial performance relative to its competitors.

The Management Problem

Until March 1992, Ahlsell had been operating like a group of eleven separate regional businesses, each having its own central warehouse and administrative and logistical support. Given the pressure on costs at that time, the company realized that it could make substantial savings and operational improvements by cutting out the regional level. Accordingly, the warehouses and the administration and logistical support were all centralized, while the sales organization was decentralized and greater responsibility and autonomy given to local units. The number of regions was reduced, and their role was changed to one of providing coaching and support. Product specialists are now located at the regional level to support front-line units. Ahlsell has learned many lessons from its experience and has subsequently developed a slick process for rolling out the model in companies it acquires.

How Abandoning Budgets Has Enabled the Devolution of Performance Responsibility

Ahlsell's leaders recognized that the existing budgeting process was conflicting with its desire for more empowerment at the level of front-line sales units, and that budgets cost too much and added too little value. Accordingly, it further developed its management processes and scrapped the budgets. This has helped to change the culture from "push" (driven by a centrally approved plan) to "pull" (local customer demand drawing through) and has turned Ahlsell into a more responsive organization.

GOVERNANCE FRAMEWORK.   There are no detailed sales plans made centrally. Only general aims are communicated from above. Units are free to develop their own approaches in response to local conditions and customer demands. The new organization recognizes that all business is local, and customer relationships are forged through front-line units. The aim of these units is to attract and retain customers and conduct profitable business. They have a high degree of autonomy. They can decide about recruiting or terminating staff, salary levels, customer discounts, and even whether to obtain supplies through the central system (if they can obtain them more cheaply by another route, they are allowed to do so). This autonomy and involvement in local decision making builds commitment to success. The local team owns its goals.

Staff turnover is less than 5 percent per annum overall (lower than the industry norm), and in plumbing and heating (the longest-running business area) it is markedly lower than the competition. The company believes that managers and staff like to work in an environment where they have more responsibility and greater freedom to act. Not only are individuals' capabilities stretched, but they also develop more as businesspeople. Both lead to increased job satisfaction and higher levels of motivation. Underpinning this culture of responsibility is the trust that senior executives place in local people. They believe that a clear set of principles and values enables local managers to make decisions with confidence. Local managers know the strategy of the firm and how they fit within it. They know costs and profitability. They know operating boundaries, including which customer belongs to which branch.

There is no fixed performance contract to undermine the system. At the end of each year, unit managers (not staff, but there are many managers) receive a bonus for the period. This is based on the performance of the unit relative to the previous year's performance (based on return on sales).

PERFORMANCE CLIMATE.   Ahlsell now sets the industry standards in terms of profitability. It began by identifying the critical success factors for the business overall as well as for its profit centers, and then chose appropriate measures for them. In the central warehouse, for example, the key measures chosen were cost per line item, costs as a percentage of turnover, stock availability, level of service, picked lines per hour, and stock turnover rate. Managers now set relative targets based on internal benchmarks (for example, by looking at trends and comparing the performance of different product groups) and on external benchmarks (by comparing performance with other companies).

The key measures chosen for the front-line sales units were growth in profitability, return on sales (RoS), efficiency (measured as gross profit divided by salary cost), and market share. The performance of all units is ranked in league tables that are visible to everyone. The top league ("The Premier League") includes units with a return on sales in excess of the set benchmark. Members are measured on both growth in net profit and return on sales. The next league ("The Qualifiers") includes units that fall short of the baseline target. They are measured just on RoS.

The impact on performance can best be seen when new acquisitions are exposed to the leagues for the first time. Managers new to the culture who previously thought they were performing reasonably well are both surprised and bemused as to why they should be so far behind existing Ahlsell units. This drives them forward. "If they can do it then so can we" is their response. They thus endeavor to find out what they need to do to improve and work their way into the premier league.

Each month the performance of every unit is measured and league tables produced to identify the best and worst performers. The reporting system is fast and open. Everyone at every level in the company sees the results at the same time.

FREEDOM TO DECIDE.   These changes represent a major shift of power from the center and regions to front-line units. These units are now accountable for their own success. Group executives outline and communicate the overall strategic direction, goals, and targets (e.g., one objective was to become number one in the plumbing and heating products field within two years). Within these parameters, local units are free to work out their own strategies and respond to opportunities and threats in the way they think best. Units are also expected to achieve the "standard" level of gross margin and to outperform each other, but no specific targets are set. Planning and improvement is a continuous process, not just a once-a-year exercise.

Units are expected to use the information system to control their own performance. There are no remote business controllers who will do the job for them. The exceptions (where performance is not up to standard) stand out clearly. There is no place to hide. The culture is one of rewarding success and learning from mistakes. Recognition is an important part of the process. In addition to awarding "red roses" to staff in the best-performing unit, that unit may also be featured in the in-house journal that is published six times a year.

There is no annual capital expenditure plan. Investment proposals are dealt with as and when requirements arise. Gunnar Haglund says that "they come when they come." Each is treated on its merits, with no fixed hurdle rate. There is no budget at Ahlsell, and no annual allocation of resources. Units increase or reduce resource levels in response to changing demands, but are accountable for their gross margin. Thus they endeavor to manage their costs within a cost-to-income KPI. Units are also free to find their own sources of supply for products for resale, if they can secure them at lower cost than through the central system.

TEAM-BASED RESPONSIBILITY.   While warehousing, distribution and logistics management were centralized, sales were decentralized and responsibility devolved to front-line teams. Whereas there had previously been fourteen profit centers, the number was greatly expanded by making each business area team (e.g., heating and plumbing) within each local unit a separate profit center. There are now over two hundred profit centers (or "sales units") in the company at its 120 establishments. This has enabled the company to introduce internal performance league tables that act as the primary spur to continuous performance improvement.

CUSTOMER ACCOUNTABILITY.   The major change in performance focus was the abandonment of central plans and top-down targets. The general rule now is that front-line units manage the relationship with all customers in their locality. When a customer is doing business in more than one unit or region, sales continue to be counted as belonging to the units where the sales occur, but the responsibility for making price agreements is placed in the unit or region where the headquarters of the customer is based or, in the case of national accounts, with the corporate center. Customers feel that front-line units are more responsive. One principle is customer ownership. Each customer is "owned" by a branch. Moreover, customers are managed by businesspeople who can resolve problems more quickly than in more centralized companies, which helps to keep customers loyal.

OPEN AND ETHICAL INFORMATION.   Given Ahlsell's vision of a large number of small profit centers, each having performance responsibility, leaders needed to redesign the management information systems to support decision makers at the front line. These systems were developed using the following principles:

- Teams should manage their own performance, not wait to be told what to do by others. Performance improvement within operating teams would be encouraged through internal competition, free access to information, and learning from the best.
- Reports should be specific to individual local responsibility areas.
- The people with responsibility are the ones who should analyze the results, because action will follow more quickly, and making their own discoveries should lead to greater commitment and motivation.
- Information should be distributed to everyone at the same time. Such openness among units should enable them to operate an internal benchmarking system.
- Follow-up reports should be based on a combination of nonfinancial key ratios and financial results. They should include earnings, costs, and interest on capital, to give as full a picture of performance as possible. The information should be based on a common database, and there should be just one version of the truth.
- Rolling forecasts (looking five quarters ahead) should be prepared to support decision making. (These are now prepared quarterly by staff at head office and involve telephone calls to a few key people. They only take a few days each quarter to collate and prepare.)

Ahlsell now has an information system based on the highest ethical values. As finance director Gunnar Haglund explains:

> We established at the outset that one of our key principles was self-management and internal competition based on free access to information. We reduce all management reports to the simplest and most relevant content and format. We only use real numbers. Everyone can see relative success or failure. It drives knowledge sharing and the transfer of best practices.

Conclusions

Ahlsell is consistently more profitable than its competitors. One of the reasons is that its employees are more satisfied. This leads to higher levels of satisfied customers, who are more loyal and profitable. Another reason is that its costs are lower and profit margins higher. The key drivers are a cost-effective centralized logistics system and very low levels of overhead costs at both regional and head office levels. But there are other reasons relating to its empowerment philosophy.

Managers are well attuned to local market conditions. They can set discount levels keenly. Their units are more adaptive to changes in their localities. They recruit staff or lay them off as and when required (rather than, as previously, just fitting in with an annual budget cycle) because they have the authority to set staffing levels. They find that small sales units (typically five to ten people) are easy to oversee. They can understand their profitability statements, and they know what action needs to be taken to improve performance. This performance is clearly visible and can easily be compared with others. There is a keen sense of competition among the sales units. The self-management philosophy is, "If he can do it, why can't I?"

Leyland Trucks

In 1969 over two hundred thousand trucks were produced in the U.K. Within thirty years production had fallen to less than fourteen thousand. Although trucks had been manufactured at Leyland for more than fifty years, few would have bet that the company could have survived such a catastrophic decline. The workforce had fallen from 14,000 in the 1970s to just four thousand in 1989, leaving deep scars and a lack of faith in the ability of management to secure future employment. By 1991, Leyland Trucks was profitable, and it has remained so ever since. In the year 2000 it was voted the best engineering factory in the United Kingdom. The key was the implementation of a business philosophy based on empowering front-line teams. Anyone who can remember the internecine warfare between managers and labor unions at British Leyland in the 1970s will understand the extent of this transformation.

The Management Problem

In the mid-1980s, Leyland Trucks was acquired by Dutch company DAF, and in 1989 John Oliver was persuaded to rejoin the company as CEO. He had previously been with the company from 1972 to 1986. On his return he was pleasantly surprised at the strength of the management team but was equally dismayed that the old attitudes of "them versus us" remained entrenched. He joined the company at a critical time. Whereas 1989 was a (relative) boom year for trucks, 1990 saw a collapse in the market. Something drastic had to be done.

How Abandoning Budgets Enabled
Devolution of Performance Responsibility

Oliver's vision was one of empowerment, with the performance management process being changed to allow this process to happen effectively. Though budgets remained in place, the fixed performance contract was abandoned. "Once we had agreed [on] the budget, we put it away in a drawer. It was useless as a basis for managing the business," notes human resources director Charlie Poskett. The empowerment project was called "Team Enterprise."

GOVERNANCE FRAMEWORK. The empowerment philosophy at Leyland Trucks recognizes that motivation is much more concerned with sharing common goals (e.g., maintaining job security) and being involved in the improvement efforts of the team than with financial incentives. That is why all piecework and other "payment by results" systems on the shop floor were eventually abandoned (despite resistance from the labor unions). Recognition became particularly important. Simple thank you cards for doing a good job and sending birthday cards to all employees have an impact far beyond the cost and effort involved. Using celebrities and customers to hand out certificates and awards is another powerful way of recognizing achievement.

PERFORMANCE CLIMATE.   Abandoning the fixed performance contract was a key change in the Leyland transformation. As Oliver notes:

> Team Enterprise demands a holistic view of the world of work from all of our employees. We want them to be concerned about output quality, productivity, and customer delight. And then we want them to give their attention to safety, to the environment, and to working with colleagues right across the organization. . . . We want a purer form of motivation to support this involvement.
>
> Unfortunately, piecework systems come from different times. If people are paid by results, that's exactly what will dominate their daily thinking. They will focus exclusively on getting as many widgets out of the door as possible to maximize their earnings. Once the requisite number has been achieved you can forget about everything else. Quality, customer satisfaction, on-time delivery, and so on do not figure in their personal vocabularies. Job-and-finish mentalities can often free up huge tranches of spare time but, in their minds, that's theirs. They've earned it, so you can't have it. Managers may tear their hair out with frustration, seeing this huge window of opportunity for addressing all the other ills of working life. But we shouldn't blame the workers. Management created the system, management created the values, and management have to accept total responsibility for the situation.[2]

There is a strong competitive element in the new group. The U.S. owner of Leyland Trucks, PACCAR, has eight plants in the United States and Europe, and league tables drive performance improvement using such measures as health and safety, productivity, quality, staff turnover, and absentee levels. There is also recognition for good performance. For example, there is a "President's prize" for best plant and there are awards for highest quality, most improved plant, and so forth.

FREEDOM TO DECIDE.   Moving to a delayered structure eliminated 42 percent of all senior and middle management positions within two years. Within four years, the figure had risen to 56 percent. In other words, as Oliver explains, for the same deliverables, only 44 managers out of 100 remained after just four years.[3] With the shift to a one team attitude with shared values, teams now challenge any wasteful activities in their constant search for improvement. The suggestion scheme ("every little bit counts") has been a real success, and it is from these suggestions that many wasteful activities have been identified and acted upon.

An example of how everyone bought into strategic change was the "zero cost growth" initiative—a declaration that the company had to grow significantly to survive, but that this growth had to be achieved with zero additional fixed cost and only marginal incremental variable cost. It meant, for example, that future pay raises had to be earned through productivity growth. The key issue was that the responsibility for achieving this objective was *everybody's*.

Strategy is not fixed. Monthly and quarterly forecasts indicate whether there needs to be a strategy review. Group managers will only seek reasonable answers to assure themselves that such changes are justified. There is now a strong degree of trust and confidence between group-level and local teams.

TEAM BASED RESPONSIBILITY.   Significant responsibility has now been devolved to self-managed teams. But senior managers recognized that it was vital that authority and freedom to act be balanced by ability and responsibility. This balancing act is generally carried out by a combination of the business unit manager and the business unit technician. Each business unit manager is responsible for one hundred and twenty direct operators. With such limited scope to intervene, the role of the business unit technician becomes important. The responsibilities of these technicians are designed to generate a multifunctional support capability for the various teams in their domain. The ideal skills matrix would be a balance of quality, tooling, people management, method improvement, and logistics.[4] The result of the new structure is that 85 percent of day-to-day problems occurring on the assembly lines are addressed by line-based technicians, with only the remaining 15 percent requiring the attention of a technical expert.[5]

Teams are made up of around sixteen to eighteen members. The original design attributed significant responsibility to the team leader, or "key operator," as he or she was known. This was a major mistake. Capabilities needed to be spread around the team. Oliver explains:

> Basically, our mistake was in expecting too much from the key operator. With hindsight, it is obvious that if traditional supervision couldn't hack it, then there was little reason to suppose that the key operator wouldn't equally struggle given the same load under much the same conditions. Our basic model was flawed. We didn't need one key influencer in the group—we needed a bunch! . . . We set about creating a "critical mass" within each team. One team member was assigned responsibility for health and safety; another might take on training; a third, housekeeping; and so on. By subdividing the responsibilities and spreading them across the team, we improved the critical mass of team members who were actively involved in managing the process.[6]

CUSTOMER ACCOUNTABILITY.   Teams see themselves as part of a seamless network that serves the end customer. This philosophy also extends to the supply chain. This is vital because most of the key parts for trucks are built externally and thus must arrive at the appropriate time and to the exact specification. Moving from a make-for-stock system with a typical lead time of twelve to fourteen weeks to a build-to-order system with a lead time of four to five weeks was thought to be impossible. There was resistance everywhere. The sales force thought it was crazy, and the assembly plants thought it was an equally hair-brained idea.

Oliver relates the impact of this change:

> In 1989, this would have been impossible to contemplate. In those days, we still operated a monthly cycle where virtually nothing was delivered in the first three weeks, followed by an almighty crush in the last week before cut-off. The final weekend of the cycle was not one that any senior manager should witness, as it resembled sheer chaos. However, with the advent of Team Enterprise, we had not just moved to weekly controlled delivery, we were well on the way to daily predictability. . . . The end result was that the Leyland plant pioneered the scheme and handled the change magnificently—so

successfully in fact that ultimately a "fast-track" service was offered which turned urgent orders around in just two or three weeks.[7]

Oliver goes on to estimate the financial impact: "I would estimate conservatively that the cash saving for Leyland alone [is] at least £40m plus ongoing cost reductions in excess of £4m [per annum]."[8]

Achieving a throughput of sixty trucks per day results in a highly profitable operation and secure employment for everyone. Thus, accommodating fast-track orders and working extra hours are all part of the social contract that now exists in the firm.

OPEN AND ETHICAL INFORMATION.   All information concerning performance and scheduling is open and shared with teams. Indeed, this was identified at the outset as a key part of the devolution process. Without fast and open information, how would teams be able to identify and deal with problems? How would they be able to adapt to fast-track orders entering the system?

Measures are geared to self-managed teams at the plant level. When you walk around the plant, you are aware of electronic "ticker tape" notice boards that display the latest output, quality, safety, and productivity figures, and even employee birthdays. Graphs and charts fill notice boards. Every Tuesday there is a written brief (not missed in ten years) that tells employees about performance achievement. And twice a year there is a business review that includes the entire workforce. Every employee completes a satisfaction survey once every fourteen months and has his or her training needs assessed.

Conclusions

The transformation of Leyland Trucks illustrates how behavior and performance can be completely turned on their head by unifying the whole organization behind a clear purpose, shared values and commitments, a focus on satisfying customers, and fair rewards. By involving the whole workforce in improving competitiveness, the company was able to survive and prosper against all the odds—and the odds were very long. Radical devolution is only possible and sustainable if it does not collide with top-down financially driven performance targets. Even then it is extremely hard work. But the rewards are higher than almost any other management change program around.

Leyland Trucks has proved that the (significant) benefits of empowerment can happen within a few years. However, it also demonstrated that empowerment cannot be given; it can only be taken. And it has proved that recognition systems are one of the most powerful yet underutilized tools in the management toolbox.

Svenska Handelsbanken

The Handelsbanken management model introduced by Dr. Jan Wallander in the early 1970s is predicated on the belief that the only sustainable competitive advantage available to a firm in a fast-changing world (especially in a service business) lies with its *people*—especially their creativity, insights, and judgment—a model in vivid contrast to the numbers-driven alternative so prevalent elsewhere.

The Management Problem

Prior to Wallander joining the bank, it operated with a traditional multidivisional model in which senior managers were the fountains of knowledge, strategic planners, and resource allocators; middle managers were the controllers who connected executives with the front line; and front-line managers were the implementers. Budgets defined power, authority, and one's place in the hierarchy. They enabled executives to manage capital. And planning, coordinating, and controlling detailed actions became the key management processes. It was this model that Wallander wanted to change. He believed that it supported a centralized bureaucracy, slowed down decisions, increased costs, and created a culture of dependency.

The changing environment was another reason why annual budgets were no longer the right tools for the performance management job. Wallander recognized that the bank's future success would rest on six factors: its ability to satisfy shareholders consistently, to improve the capabilities of its people, to introduce a self-questioning and improvement-oriented culture, to reduce costs and increase quality, to find and keep the right customers, and to maintain the highest ethical standards.

How Abandoning Budgets Enabled Devolution of Performance Responsibility

Managers do not engage in any formal strategy process, nor do they prepare and approve annual plans (short or long term) or budgets. Chairman Arne Mårtensson, like Wallander, believes that "budgeting and long-range planning often do more harm than good, not only because of the time and resources wasted. They also block the thinking and make quick adoption difficult when the time is right. In our bank we have replaced budgeting with a good accounting system."

GOVERNANCE FRAMEWORK.   Wallander knew that successful implementation of his new management ideas would depend on capable and committed people. Any disaffection would be a major problem. He believed that in order to get a first-class job out of people, a necessary prerequisite is that they feel involved in what they are doing, so that what they get out of their jobs is not only money but also a feeling of satisfaction. He wanted Handelsbanken employees to enjoy real freedom, yet there must also be self-discipline and order throughout the firm's operations. This web of interconnectedness and self-regulation is woven around a set of values and principles with a clear organizational purpose at its core. This sense of purpose is above and beyond shareholder returns. It is set out in the annual report in these terms: "Handelsbanken aims to make a better contribution to society than other banks. This should be done by offering a better service while using fewer of society's resources, i.e. by having lower costs. If we succeed in this we will also achieve higher profitability. This is why our goal is to have higher profitability than comparable banks."

These principles and values set the framework for local decision making across the organization. There are no mission statements and annual plans to cloud the issue. All employees are expected to understand the parameters within which they must work and to make decisions accordingly—and they are trusted to do so. The central management team works very closely with the regions and branches. For example, the CEO's visits to regions form a crucial two-way communication, with clarity of standards and policies flowing down and market intelligence flowing up.

Wallander also had a belief that people must be involved in setting their own improvement plans. In other words, if any target or plan is imposed on a person or team, then little or no ownership of it, or commitment to it, will result. No one can be persuaded of someone else's view of the future. Individuals must engage in the planning process with others and thus share in the commitment of the team. This view is fundamental to understanding Wallander's philosophy.

PERFORMANCE CLIMATE.　Wallander believed that beating the competition should pervade every aspect of performance management at Handelsbanken. As he explained, relative measures are more effective than stretch targets because they are always current and keep moving the mean upward:

> We just communicate to people the average and a ranking that
> shows which branches are above and which are below. The system
> works on its own. Senior executives don't need to push people, they
> just advise. Managers know "what is acceptable performance"—
> you can't linger in the depths of the league table for long! Of course
> it also relies on high levels of trust and motivation. Our managers
> can do anything to improve performance. Peer pressure plays an
> important part in this process. No branch manager wants to let
> down the regional team, and as they speak to each other all the
> time, there is both pressure to perform and a willingness to help
> each other. It is this tension between internal competition and
> cooperative support that enables us to keep improving.

Wallander reinforced this competitive performance climate by introducing a series of "presidential visits" that occur throughout the year, in which the chief executive spends two days with a region and its branches. During this visit the CEO challenges regional and branch managers on their performance assumptions and how they can improve. This is an important part of the "stretch" thinking that the bank tries hard to encourage. But it is the sense of real competition that continues day in and day out between regional banks and between branches within a region that really drives improved performance. It works on its own and does not depend on any arbitrary targets to drive improvement.

FREEDOM TO DECIDE.   Successful devolution also requires discipline at every level. Resisting the temptation to interfere is crucial. It is easy to allow centralization to return through the back door. Issuing memos, instructions, and directives is a symptom of centralizing forces and must be resisted. To support the new approach at Handelsbanken, a policy decision was taken not to issue any more head office directives or reports. As Wallander noted, "No one missed them. Many central staff were quite shocked when life carried on as normal."

Branch managers decide the level of branch resources. Managerial authority was extended in the early 1990s to include decisions on staffing levels, and more recently on staff salaries and negotiations for property leases. The reason for including staff resources within the manager's scope is that if customer demand falls or if the new IT systems release branch resources, it is managers who are best placed to decide whether to hold on to staff or release them. The results of this extension of the empowerment process surprised everyone. Far from staff numbers increasing (as most expected), numbers decreased as managers took a more realistic view of future performance.

Mårtensson captured the essence of these changes:

> There is no scope for sweet-talking away bad results. The figures should speak, and speak clearly for themselves. The branch is responsible for its profitability and has the power to change what needs to be changed. We operate many a profitable branch in small villages with just a few hundred inhabitants. While most banks have devolved authority to regions, we have taken it much further, that is, down to branch level. This goes a long way to explaining our cost advantage. Other banks have access to the same technology, so the difference must be down to how we work. Radical decentralization can only work with fast and open information systems that provide effective multilevel controls. We are quick to spot any changes in trends within regions and branches and this leads to searching questions being asked on the telephone. Problems are transparent; they are not hidden within the nooks and crannies of management layers and allowed to fester.

TEAM-BASED RESPONSIBILITY.   Wallander believed that the people best placed to make operating decisions were those closest to the customer, so he wanted to establish a strategy and an action planning process that was devolved to regions and branches. This would be a continuous process with no set plan to constrain actions. His idea was that "the branch is the bank" and that branch managers should "run their own business" within a number of operating parameters. They have thus created some six hundred profit centers in the bank, including the branches and central service units. Though they have flexibility over prices, discounts, and which products they sell, they also know that costs must be around 40 percent of income and that each member of the staff must contribute to profit.

Branch teams are expected to maximize their profitability within the framework of the bank's management policies. Well-trained and capable people acting on their own don't need much supervision, and thus many of the costs associated with a large control-oriented organization are rendered superfluous. There are now only three layers from branch manager to regional manager to chief executive. This results in very wide spans of control with no possibility for micromanagement. There is no written organization chart. Any decisions that cannot be taken at the front line are escalated almost immediately, and an answer will normally be available within twenty-four hours.

CUSTOMER ACCOUNTABILITY.   One of Wallander's most important changes was to abolish the internal "please the boss" style of management. In effect, he changed the management structure to look more like an inverted pyramid (figure 6-1), with the CEO and the head office groups supporting the regions and branches. While regions employ specialist advisers, including legal and human resource people, branch managers report directly to the regional manager. The emphasis is on clear lines of responsibility. There is no matrix management. Managers have responsibility for financial results and can take whatever action they deem appropriate to improve them. Regions and branches are clearly established as profit centers. They face the customer (either internal or external) and are geared to respond rapidly to individual customer requests. Telephone and Internet banking are seen as extensions of the branch network and are made to appear seamless through the IT system.

FIGURE 6 - 1

Inverting the Pyramid at Handelsbanken

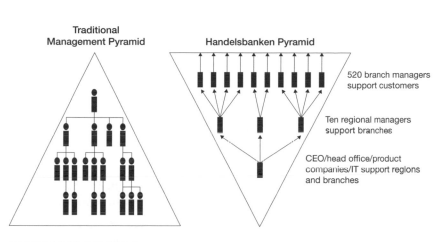

Traditional
Management Pyramid

Handelsbanken Pyramid

520 branch managers
support customers

Ten regional managers
support branches

CEO/head office/product
companies/IT support regions
and branches

Note: Figure is not drawn to scale.

In contrast to the approach of many other financial services companies, there is no emphasis on central marketing or on meeting product targets. Whereas the product-led approach (with its supporting IT system) tells managers a lot about product sales, product profitability, and perhaps the market share of individual products, it tells them very little about customers, their changing financial circumstances, and their changing requirements. Mårtensson explains:

> The selection of the right customers determines the productivity and profitability of the branch. Making a telephone call now and then, or a spontaneous visit, or sending a birthday flower or a personal letter to mark a special occasion are all ways of keeping in contact with the customer. You do not usually lose a customer because of high prices. You lose them because they are not valued. When we study branches with low cost-to-income ratios it becomes apparent that they seek out customers that don't require lots of time expended on them. This emphasis on selecting each individual customer is also the reason why we do not offer particularly advantageous terms for special groups such as students, retired people, or shareholders. We should offer good customers good

terms and conditions, and it is the branch that decides who is a good customer.

OPEN AND ETHICAL INFORMATION.   Wallander knew that fast, open, and shared information is the oxygen that supports the decentralized organization. But he also knew that confidence in the numbers is paramount. He therefore developed a number of important principles and practices that underpin accountability:

- Profit centers are provided with online information on branch and customer profitability, together with acquisitions and defections.
- Every customer should be attached to one branch irrespective of where transactions take place. The accounting system should transfer all income and expenditure to the appropriate branch, but with some credit to the branch where the transaction took place.
- All cost center products and services are charged to investment/profit centers. In other words, cost centers should break even each year. The reason is that profit center managers must see the burden of these costs even though some of them are not within their sphere of influence.
- All transfer charges are at cost. There should be no element of profit included in the transfer price; otherwise, the numbers will risk losing credibility.
- Charges are based on transactions or on some other agreed-upon basis (if transaction charging is not feasible). Service agreements set the service standards that must be met.
- Investment centers are charged for the capital they use.

All managers receive information at the same time. Group controller Ulf Hamrin explains the value of this approach:

> At head office we don't use the system to micro-manage front-line operations. We monitor and observe transaction volumes, customer gains and losses, customer profits, branch profits, cost patterns, productivity, and much more. If I see a branch underperforming I will send an e-mail to a colleague in the region (there is

one controller in each regional bank), who will make a suggestive call to the branch. That's all that happens—it is then up to the branch whether or not to take action. This system, of course, depends on an effective and fast information system. We can monitor region and branch profitability on-line. This enables us to see patterns and blips and tells us when to stick our finger in the pie. For example, we can spot patterns of excess discounts, defecting customers, product sales, and unusual transaction volumes.

It is sometimes said that decentralized operations come with a price—loss of control. This is not the case at Handelsbanken. In fact, the control system is multifaceted, rich in content, and places managers at every level in a strong position to take early action should this be necessary.

Conclusions

Handelsbanken has consistently produced better profits than its Nordic rivals for the past thirty years. Its competitive advantage cannot be easily explained by conventional economic wisdom. The difference has to be the way it manages its business. We can see the extent of these results by looking at the six success factors we identified in chapter 1.

- *Sustainable value creation.* Basing its competitive advantage on people rather than products has meant that Handelsbanken has produced consistent returns to shareholders (24 percent compound total shareholder return over the last twenty-two years to 2001—33 percent higher than its nearest rival). Earnings per share growth of 10.9 percent compound for the period 1990 to 2000 is equally impressive. Handelsbanken is also a safe stock. Its Moody's rating (Aa2) is the third highest in Europe.
- *Attracting and keeping capable and committed people.* Talented graduates want to join Handelsbanken more than any other financial services company in Sweden, not because it offers the highest salaries and benefits but because young managers are expected to run their own business within a radically decentralized structure. Employee turnover is extremely low (around 3 percent), reflecting high levels of satisfaction (layoffs are unknown). Managers are not easily poached. It has been said

that a figure in excess of 30 to 40 percent extra would be required to attract a Handelsbanken employee to another bank.

- *Continuous innovation.* Handelsbanken was voted the joint best Internet bank in Europe in 2000. Forty-five percent of all corporate customers and 25 percent of private customers use its Internet banking services. One of the bank's principles is "not to copy others." In other words, being different is a strength; there is no better evidence of this than its innovative approach to the management model itself.

- *Permanent low costs and high quality.* Empowered people don't need much supervision. Nor do they need the extensive central services that most organizations provide. This has a dramatic impact on the cost structure. Using the two key measures of costs to total assets and cost to income, Handelsbanken is by far the most cost-efficient bank in Europe. It achieved a cost-to-income ratio of 45 percent in 2001, compared with over 60 percent for most international banks. One reason is that costs are constantly challenged rather than protected by the budgeting system; another is that bad debts are exceptionally low, largely due to the bank's policy of devolving credit responsibility to front-line people.

- *Customer loyalty.* It is perhaps because branches "own" their customers (no matter where transactions take place) and because employees can make fast decisions and provide customized solutions that Handelsbanken has low staff turnover and the lowest number of customer complaints in its sector, and consistently tops the customer satisfaction charts in Sweden.

- *Ethical reporting practices.* Although Handelsbanken has comprehensive internal audit procedures, the real internal controls come from the openness of its information systems. Performance is transparent at every level, and any problems are immediately obvious.

Chapter Summary

This chapter described how three organizations have used adaptive processes to empower their front-line people:

- Ahlsell is a Swedish wholesaler with sales of around $1 billion. The creation of over two hundred profit centers and the devolution of responsibility to unit managers were among the key changes that led to its success.
- Leyland Trucks is a U.K. truck manufacturer (now part of the U.S.-based PACCAR group). The story of the transformation of Leyland Trucks is about how behavior and performance can be completely turned on their heads by unifying the whole organization behind a clear purpose, shared values and commitments, a focus on satisfying customers, and fair rewards.
- Svenska Handelsbanken is the consummate beyond budgeting case. Dr. Wallander had a clear vision of an adaptive and devolved organization within which regions and branches would be accountable for competitive results. He approached his task by spending time talking to managers and employees across the company about the principles of decentralization. He then abandoned budgeting at a stroke. Since that time, Handelsbanken has maintained a significant cost advantage over all its rivals.

Chapter Seven

Principles of Radical Decentralization

> Only if a decision would substantially damage the organization is the manager entitled to intervene. In aviation, the trainer allows the pilot to get it wrong provided that the mistake will not crash the plane. It is the only way the trainee will learn to fly alone.[1]
>
> —CHARLES HANDY

Effective empowerment is the product of freedom multiplied by capability. As with any mathematical equation, if one of the variables is zero, the result will also be zero. This explains why so many attempts at empowerment fail. Few leaders seem capable of supporting both variables at the same time. This is what distinguishes leaders at firms such as Ahlsell, Leyland Trucks, and Handelsbanken from the rest of the pack. The result has been significant and *sustainable* success.

The evidence from our cases is that there are six principles that leaders should adopt:

1. Provide a governance framework based on clear principles and boundaries.
2. Create a high-performance climate based on relative success.

3. Give people freedom to make local decisions that are consistent with governance principles and the organization's goals.
4. Place the responsibility for value creating decisions on front-line teams.
5. Make people accountable for customer outcomes.
6. Support open and ethical information systems that provide "one truth" throughout the organization.

Figure 7-1 shows the effects of these principles. A clear governance framework leads to the acceptance of local decision making by front-line teams throughout the organization. A high-performance climate leads to sustained competitive success. The freedom to decide fosters innovation and responsiveness. Team-based responsibility results in a greater focus on creating value and reducing waste. Customer accountability builds more commitment to satisfying customers profitably. Finally, an information culture based on openness and one truth promotes ethical behavior.

FIGURE 7 - 1

Using Beyond Budgeting Principles to Radically Decentralize the Organization

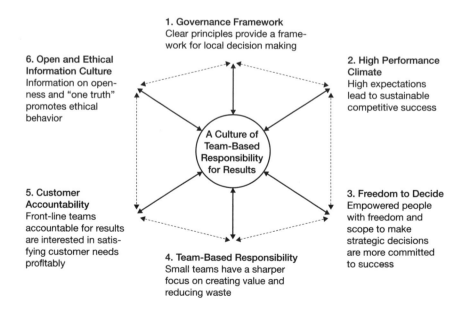

1. Governance Framework
Clear principles provide a frame-work for local decision making

6. Open and Ethical Information Culture
Information on open-ness and "one truth" promotes ethical behavior

2. High Performance Climate
High expectations lead to sustainable competitive success

A Culture of Team-Based Responsibility for Results

5. Customer Accountability
Front-line teams accountable for results are interested in satis-fying customer needs profitably

3. Freedom to Decide
Empowered people with freedom and scope to make strategic decisions are more committed to success

4. Team-Based Responsibility
Small teams have a sharper focus on creating value and reducing waste

This chapter looks at the common principles that leaders have used to transform their organizations.

Principle 1: Provide a Governance Framework Based on Clear Principles and Boundaries

It is not difficult to see why the budgeting process is such a barrier to effective empowerment. It restricts decision making to specified plans and budgets, and it assumes the absence of trust. To remove these barriers to empowerment, leaders should (1) provide clear principles and boundaries, (2) bind people to a common purpose and shared values, and (3) adopt a "coach and support" leadership style.

Provide Clear Principles and Boundaries

In every organization, people at all levels need clear guidelines so they know what they can and cannot do. Whereas in the control-oriented organization these were based on mission statements, plans, and budgets, in the empowered organization they are based on clear principles, values, and boundaries. Essential boundaries include the strategic domain and the codes of conduct and ethical and environmental considerations within which managers can operate, the time between reporting intervals, and the discretionary area between what managers must do and what they might do. In the empowered organization, people are empowered to make mistakes and equally empowered to fix them.

At Borealis, leaders know that the new management style can only operate effectively if there is high trust supported by open information. But if this trust is breached, then the sanctions are clear—people will not survive. Notes Bogsnes: "We are ruthless on policy violations. They usually lead to dismissal. We have a simple 'ethics test' so that people know whether or not their action is acceptable. They just need to ask the following question: Is it acceptable if the results of their actions appear on the front page of the newspaper? If yes, go ahead. If no, don't do it."

As we have noted, customer ownership is a key boundary issue. At firms such as Ahlsell and Handelsbanken, branches own customers whatever their size. Most customers (especially large ones) want to talk to decision makers. Whereas in most organizations these are at the regional or head office, at Handelsbanken they are at the branch. Some large customers find this difficult at first (they want to talk to someone at the head office). Not all accept it, but those that do usually build a strong local relationship that invariably leads to increased satisfaction and longer-term profitability.

Clear policies and principles provide a protective shield against unscrupulous practices, particularly if pressure is applied from a higher level. Pressure invariably arises from the need to meet fixed performance contracts. This indeed was the case at two high-profile cases (Kidder Peabody and Barings Bank).[2] Such problems are less likely to occur inside adaptive and devolved companies because there is no direct connection between fixed targets and rewards. This disconnection strengthens the whole governance process.

Bind People to a Common Purpose and Shared Values

Although many of the organizations we have examined have produced exceptional returns for shareholders, none of them states that creating shareholder value is its overarching purpose. Instead, leaders endeavor to bind people to a cause rather than some nebulous mission statement, plan, or budget. Handelsbanken aims to make a better contribution to society than other banks by offering a better service while using fewer of society's resources (that is, by having lower costs). This provides a clear and rational reason for being for all employees. Wealth creation is necessary and has a social purpose. Each generation of Handelsbanken leaders seeks to leave the organization in better shape than when they inherited it. Pride and passion are values that everyone can identify with.

IKEA is another firm totally committed to leading by setting a clear purpose, inviolate principles, and shared values. The driving force for success is not so much profit but improving the quality of life for as many people as possible. Such words as *humility, modesty, responsibility, simplicity,* and *enthusiasm* populate the IKEA vocabulary. Reacting to the cartel-like agreements among Swedish furniture manufacturers and retailers that kept furniture prices beyond the reach of young people trying to set up their first homes, Ingvar Kamprad, the founder of IKEA, started his company in 1953 not only to exploit a business opportunity (and create wealth for shareholders) but also to tackle a social problem.

Adopt a "Coach and Support" Leadership Style

Empowerment is unlikely to work unless leaders become coaches and mentors rather than commanders and controllers. Handelsbanken uses a coaching style of management. Even if senior managers can see at first hand that poor decisions are being made, all they will do is send an e-mail or make a brief phone call to inquire about the problem. It is up to the local manager to react. This discipline by leaders not to interfere is one of the toughest elements of the empowerment process. As Chairman Arne Mårtensson has noted, "You have to learn to keep your hands down by your side even when you could intervene and help solve a problem."

Trust and confidence take time to build, however. Handelsbanken (now over thirty years into its devolution program) has driven decision making down to front-line branch office staff, but Fokus Bank (only six years into a similar program) has only devolved similar decisions to regional staff. These contrasting positions capture the progressive steps that empowerment takes as managers grow into their new roles and confidence matures.

Principle 2: Create a High-Performance Climate Based on Relative Success

As we noted in chapter 6, most senior executives are fixated on meeting the numbers at every quarter- and year-end. This pervasive obsession drives dysfunctional and disruptive behavior at every level. Alternatively, as seen in our cases, managing without fixed targets and incentives can lead to strong *and consistent* levels of performance. But this style of management needs the support of leaders who (1) champion relative performance, (2) challenge ambition, and (3) balance competition and cooperation.

Champion Relative Performance

Fixed performance contracts tie operating managers to specific agreements and reduce their flexibility. Breaking free from these contracts is perhaps the single most important step that leaders can take to create a culture of empowerment. Jan Wallander and Gunnar Haglund are both devout believers in relativity. Indeed, the adoption of relative measures, perhaps above anything else, was the key to replacing the budgeting culture at Handelsbanken and Ahlsell. Wallander's beliefs are rooted in his economic philosophy. "The fundamental purpose of a firm in a market economy," he believes, "is to deliver as high a return on capital invested in the company as possible. A company is successful and will survive if it gives a higher return than other companies in the same field. The real target is thus not an absolute sum in dollars and cents but a relative one. Beating the competition is the real target."

Challenge Ambition

All the leaders in the companies we examined had great ambition and spent much of their time challenging their people. This isn't just about new products and strategies but about rethinking every element of their concept of business. In other words, it is about *thinking differently*. It's about insight and collaboration. Dismantling the budgeting model and clearing away the rubble of industrial age management practices are perfect examples. When asked at an interview what was the new role of the CEO in this empowered management model, Handelsbanken Chairman Arne Mårtensson replied, "I spend much of my time visiting regions and branches and challenging teams to improve their performance."

Balance Competition and Cooperation.

Fostering internal competition and cooperation is a delicate balancing act. Leaders don't want to create competitive teams that become archenemies as they fight for customers and resources. Handelsbanken overcame this potential problem by making an overarching rule that every customer be attached to a branch; thus, there would be no debate as to who would gain the benefit of customer orders. In practice, the opposite benefit happened: Branches shared information about customers, knowing that there were clear and inviolable boundaries. The other key decision at Handelsbanken was to create a companywide profit-sharing pool. Again, this defused any notion of gaining financial advantage by beating internal competitors. While it was peer pressure that provided the motivation to win, it was profit sharing and customer ownership that encouraged people to share knowledge.

Principle 3: Give People Freedom to Make Local Decisions that are Consistent with Governance Principles and the Organization's Goals

The central planning and budgeting process assumes that managers' have the capability to "predict and control" future outcomes. Strategic plans and budgets guide and control detailed actions. Our cases have shown that although teams at every level need strategic *direction*, they don't need detailed plans (except those derived by the team to set their own course). To instill a culture of responsibility instead of dependency, leaders should (1) challenge assumptions and risks, (2) involve everyone in strategy, and (3) empower teams to make decisions.

Challenge Assumptions and Risks

Leaders don't become passive once they transfer strategy to business unit teams. Indeed, their role remains highly active. They use their time to involve themselves in the strategy development process, though their role becomes one of challenger rather than developer. In other words, they must challenge the assumptions and risks implicit in any strategy presented to them, and ensure that better alternatives are not available.

After abandoning budgeting at Bulmers, more responsibility for developing detailed strategies has been placed on the shoulders of operating managers. Whereas budgets usually meant agreeing on numbers with little thought as to how those numbers would be achieved, the new process means committing to targets and justifying to the whole management team how these targets will be met. This forces people to think deeply about the business, especially about constraints, commitments, innovation, investment, competencies, and risks. In other words, the knowledge and creativity of key managers (most of whom have been there for many years) are now being used much more productively in achieving stretch goals.

Involve Everyone in Strategy

If local managers make fast decisions to respond quickly to emerging threats and opportunities, they are bound to make some mistakes, but as most enlightened leaders would say, that's how people learn. Conversely, no matter how many times the CEO tells people that "they have all the power and authority of the chairman," they will not make strategic decisions (certainly not those that involve any risk) if they believe that they will be punished if those decisions prove to be wrong. At all the firms we examined, leaders involve the whole team in local strategy *and* the results of their decisions. Handelsbanken branch managers have regular team meetings to review the strategic issues facing them. Assembly teams at Leyland Trucks can see the results of their decisions on screens around the plant. This inclusiveness is an important part of the process and instills in every worker a sense of personal responsibility.

Empower Teams to Make Decisions

In organizations that have abandoned budgeting, leaders make managers accountable for delivering competitive results compared with internal or external benchmarks. This is much more than delegation of authority within the constraints of budgets. Handelsbanken managers at every level are accountable for competitive results and are free to decide what action is needed to achieve them. They know that if they are not performing well there is no hiding place. They cannot make excuses with the numbers. League tables showing performance rankings and the relative position of every branch and region appear every month. And at the end of the quarter and year, the regions' overall performance of the bank is similarly measured.

Principle 4: Place the Responsibility for Value Creating Decisions on Front-Line Teams

The drive for a more competitive cost base means that business units tend to get larger as they benefit from greater economies of scale. This has resulted in the closure of many smaller units across a wide range of industries over recent decades. This approach is entirely rational if you focus on achieving the lowest-cost model of business to the exclusion of other factors such as how value is created or how customers are managed. In the organizations we have reported on, however, these factors are of paramount importance. The result is that business units tend to get smaller. The objective of leaders is to create a more entrepreneurial business, and this requires multiple units that give more and younger managers the opportunities they need to create customer value. Thus, smaller units are certainly in order. Indeed, in organizations with a branch network, we saw units with an average size of about fifteen people, and indications were that these organizations intended to devolve even further (e.g., to account manager level within branches). But the size of teams is not the issue. The aim is that everyone in the organization should carry personal responsibility for his or her part in it.

The impact on the whole organization of many small teams making independent value creating decisions in response to local opportunities and events is to create in aggregate a much more *adaptive* organization. No one is waiting for the annual planning cycle to come around, for example, to allow increases or force reductions in staffing levels. The managers in every unit are continuously assessing the balance between their anticipated workloads and their capacities to handle them. This point was vividly illustrated by a branch manager at Handelsbanken who told us that he knew, at that time, that his major corporate customer was in the process of deciding whether to transfer its head office from Stockholm to London. Had this occurred it would have had a dramatic impact on his workload and possibly the viability of his branch. Clearly, such uncertainties exist to varying degrees in every branch across the network. To ensure that the bank creates maximum value, it requires therefore that every one of its local units is continuously making small local adjustments.

The contrast in a company between this devolved and adaptive approach to management on the one hand, and the traditional budget based centrally planned model on the other is as stark as the contrast between a market economy and a centrally planned one. The market economy continuously adapts to its changing environment, whereas a centrally planned economy, as history has shown, cannot cope in a complex, rapidly changing economic environment, nor does it foster entrepreneurial attitudes. One might then ask why it has taken us so long to realize that "command and control" is as outdated a model for managing our companies as it is for our national economies.

But implementing this is far from easy. Changing functional mind-sets (follow the budget) to team-based mind-sets (satisfy the customer) is a major cultural challenge, but if done successfully it can bring major benefits. Relative targets help this change of mind-set as (unlike the annual budget) they are constantly reviewed. Further, they enable managers *themselves* to set, within limits, their own short-term improvement targets. The team-based approach is well suited to involving everyone in formulating strategy (given that strategy involves thousands of decisions at every level).

To embed the philosophy of teamwork and personal responsibility into the organization, leaders should (1) create a network of small, customer-oriented teams, and (2) base recruitment on a potential employee's "fit" with the team.

Create a Network of Small, Customer-Oriented Teams

The idea of an organization as a set of interdependent human relationships is deeply embedded in the philosophy of leaders at adaptive and devolved organizations. They see their organizations as communities. These communities are composed of multiple teams that deliver customer value. Creating large numbers of small units doesn't mean wholesale restructuring, nor does it mean the disappearance of the hierarchy (although there is a lot less of it). It is the *relationships* and the *information flows* between levels and across the business that change. For example, business unit teams are solely responsible for their results and how they compare with agreed-upon benchmarks. They don't need controlling—they need supporting. And if they fail to perform consistently, then they will not survive for long.

Leaders at Handelsbanken believe that its six hundred responsibility centers provide clarity and simplicity in setting the performance management framework. Managers are exposed and must accept full accountability for their performance. Performance comparisons are easily made, and peer pressure plays a major role in driving continuous improvement. Small independent units also stimulate entrepreneurial activity and give ambitious managers the opportunities they crave. This is a virtuous circle as the most talented managers look for companies that can give them these challenging roles.

Base Recruitment on Fit with the Team

Not everyone is cut out for the kind of open management style demanded by the adaptive and devolved organization. Some managers prefer the tightly drawn rules of the hierarchy. At Handelsbanken and Ahlsell, new recruits soon learn that they are expected to use their intuition and judgment to make value-enhancing decisions. This means that they must learn how to use information and understand the dynamics of the business.

Christer Dahle, Human Resources Manager (IT) at Handelsbanken, explains his recruitment policy.

> The people we look for are those that are thinking, creative, and strong. We sell our cultural model to graduates and it always works. We tell them that we are their opportunity for advancement and they can influence how and at what pace they develop. Our recruitment is focused more on finding the right people that will neatly fit our management style rather than those with the highest technical qualifications. In the early stages of their career, all employees learn the "Handelsbanken Way" (our management philosophy). However, this is not a set of behavioral rules. There is no operating manual at Handelsbanken. People soon learn that the organization is a network and knowing people is the way to get things done. All employees are encouraged to think about strategy and improvement. Great emphasis is placed on personal responsibility especially when dealing with customers. Half the Handelsbanken staff have lending authority. This means that customers receive a fast response. Knowledge of customer needs and the ability to tailor products is another crucial element in the customer satisfaction process.

Principle 5: Make People Accountable for Customer Outcomes

Many organizations have already shed a number of management layers in their efforts to become "lean and mean." Their objective, by and large, is to move to a more networked type of organizational model. Such a model is based on a number of *interdependent* units with distributed capabilities and expertise. It recognizes that to operate with high speed and low costs, the organization must be able to locate and combine expertise across the network and bring such collective expertise together in a seamless way to provide solutions for customers. The network concept is based on essential relationships both inside and outside the organization in terms of the outcomes they owe one another. It is the model used by most firms managing without budgets. To move to this adaptive and devolved method of working, leaders should (1) enable teams to respond to customer demand, and (2) encourage teams to share knowledge across the business.

Enable Teams to Respond to Customer Demand

Significant performance responsibility has now been devolved to customer-focused units at Leyland Trucks. Leaders learned, however, that empowerment cannot be "given" to teams; it can only be "taken." In other words, teams must want to engage in the management process and accept responsibility. However, the realization (through surveys) that this is exactly what most of them *did* want took senior management by surprise. Senior managers also recognized that it was vital that authority and freedom to act be balanced by ability and responsibility.

Leaders at Ahlsell, Leyland Trucks, and Handelsbanken work on the principle of "customers first." Ahlsell managers can do whatever they think right to meet the needs of customers. However, they are responsible for achieving high performance standards in terms of return on sales. Handelsbanken abandoned central product targets and quotas many years ago. Now, apart from new product launches, almost the only marketing is at the level of the branch. Thus, local people are empowered to know and satisfy customer needs. They have the ability to put together customer solutions, and they have control over pricing. Loss leaders can be agreed upon provided the overall business case (i.e., a profitable customer account) is kept firmly in mind.

Encourage Teams to Share Knowledge across the Business

In hierarchical structures, knowledge is, more often than not, seen by employees as a source of personal power or, at the very least, security against losing their job. But to maximize the effectiveness of knowledge, leaders must change this view. To be effective, all managers within a network need the same information at the same time. Moreover, such information should be action based, be instant, and be online.

IKEA believes in an open information system and the sharing of best practices. Sharing and integration are also fostered on what chairman Ingvar Kamprad calls the "mouth to ear" basis. The company assigns "IKEA ambassadors"—specially trained by Kamprad himself not only in the company's values and culture but also in how to spread the message—to key positions in all units, both to socialize newcomers into the IKEA philosophy and to facilitate the transfer of ideas and best practices across the company's dispersed operating units.[3]

Sharing of best practices is a key element in the IKEA success story. As one IKEA executive explained, "the newly set-up stores would look at the previously developed stores and try their hardest to improve on them. One would set up a green plant department, so the next would create a clock section." It was through such an institutionalized entrepreneurial process that some of the distinguishing characteristics of the typical IKEA store emerged: supervised play areas for children featuring a large "pool" filled with red Styrofoam balls, in-store cafes serving inexpensive exotic meals such as Swedish meatballs, and fully equipped nursery and baby-changing facilities.[4]

Principle 6: Support Open and Ethical Information Systems That Provide "One Truth" throughout the Organization

Many leaders believe that information should only reach those people authorized to see it. "The risks of having a completely open system would be too great," they say. "Anyhow, how can we trust people with sensitive information? It would reach our competitors in no time at all."

The leadership challenge in adaptive and devolved organizations is to trust people with information and accept that the real control comes from anticipating what will happen next and reacting to events faster than competitors rather than from slavishly following some outdated plan or budget. To achieve this, leaders should (1) make information fast and open rather than slow and restricted and (2) set high ethical standards for the treatment of all numbers rather than allowing managers to manipulate them.

Make Information Fast and Open

Handelsbanken has based its empowerment model on fast and open information. It delivers relevant information to the right people at the right time. Such a system provides front-line managers with the capability to make fast and well-informed decisions, to effectively manage project-based strategic initiatives, and to bounce ideas around with colleagues across the company before taking important decisions. It enables support services managers to keep up to date with best practices. It enables divisional managers to see trends, patterns, and breaks in the curve long before their competitors and thus make crucial decisions regarding products and markets. And it enables senior executives to keep asking important questions concerning strategic assumptions and risks while ensuring that operating units remain within acceptable performance parameters. Above all, it helps to share knowledge throughout the company so that strategic changes can be made quickly and potential problems solved before they fester and grow.

Set High Ethical Standards for Information Flow

Leaders in adaptive and devolved organizations believe in having only one set of numbers that is transparent throughout the whole organization. Maintaining one set of books is the key to high levels of ethical practice. This is exactly what such firms as Handelsbanken and Ahlsell do. Indeed, they have an information system based on the highest ethical values.

Providing an open and honest view of future outcomes works best in a culture underpinned by trust. It is crucially important that bad news be circulated without delay. Bad news must be assimilated quickly and dealt with as a team. By so doing, local managers will not be afraid of building the results of such bad news into their forecasts—the sting will have already been taken out of them. Handelsbanken managers share bad news immediately. For example, if one branch loses a customer, it needs to either try to recover the situation and gain the help of others that might have relevant knowledge or to replace the lost business, in which case it might solicit the help of regional managers.

Chapter Summary

The evidence from our cases suggests that there are six principles that leaders should adopt to make the radically decentralized organization work effectively. Each principle has associated best practices.

1. To enable local decision making and safeguard stakeholders' interests, leaders should provide a governance framework that is based on clear principles and boundaries rather than on rules, regulations, and budgets. Best practices include:
   - Provide clear principles and boundaries.
   - Bind people to a common purpose and shared values.
   - Adopt a "coach and support" leadership style.
2. To motivate people and ensure sustainable success, leaders should create a high-performance climate that is based on relative success rather than on fixed performance contracts and fear of failure. Best practices include:
   - Champion relative performance.
   - Challenge ambition.
   - Balance internal cooperation and competition.
3. To foster innovation and responsiveness, leaders should empower front-line teams to make local decisions that are consistent with governance principles and the organization's goals rather than with rules, central plans, and the narrow self-interest of departmental goals. Best practices include:
   - Challenge assumptions and risks.
   - Involve everyone in strategy.
   - Empower teams to make decisions.
4. To increase adaptability and reduce waste, leaders should place the responsibility for value creating decisions on front-line teams rather than trying to exert control from the center. Best practices include:
   - Create a network of small, customer-oriented teams.
   - Base recruitment on fit with the team.

5. To satisfy customer needs profitably, leaders should make people accountable for *customer* outcomes rather than meeting *functional* plans and budgets. Best practices include:
   - Enable teams to respond to customer demand.
   - Encourage teams to share knowledge across the business.
6. To promote ethical behavior, leaders should support open information systems that provide one truth throughout the organization rather than having middlemen filtering information and making it available on a need-to-know basis. Best practices include:
   - Make information fast and open.
   - Set high ethical standards for information flow.

Chapter Eight

Insights into Changing Centralized Mind-Sets

> Changing something implies not just learning something new but unlearning something that is already there and possibly in the way. What most learning theories and models overlook are the dynamics of unlearning, of overcoming resistance to change. They assume that if you can just get a clear enough vision of a positive future, this is motivation enough to get new learning started.[1]
> —EDGAR SCHEIN

Changing the centralized mind-set is a tough challenge. But this is exactly what leaders in our featured cases have done. So why doesn't every firm follow suit? The answer is that it is extremely difficult. It crucially depends on rooting out the budgeting and dependency culture. The problem, more often than not, is a lack of understanding of what leaders need to do to make empowerment work effectively. For example, they need to abandon fixed performance contracts, command-and-control management, the dependency culture, central resource allocation, the multilayered functional hierarchy, and closed information systems.

Judging by our cases, a number of issues are common to a successful transition. These include the following:

- *Selling the benefits:* How the soft numbers become hard.
- *Changing processes precedes the devolution of responsibility:*
  The order is crucial.
- *Devolving responsibility:* It cannot be "given," only "taken."
- *Overcoming the resistors:* The forces of centralization are never
  far away.
- *Letting go:* It's the ultimate challenge.
- *Changing recognition and rewards:* It's the seminal moment.
- *Maintaining the momentum:* It's a never-ending process.

Selling the Benefits: How the Soft Numbers Become Hard

In all our work with the Beyond Budgeting Round Table, we have rarely encountered the problem of convincing people that the centralized system of planning and control and the dysfunctional behavior driven by the fixed performance contract need changing. Nor have we found it difficult to convince people that budgets do a poor job of providing hard-pressed managers with the steering mechanisms they need to run the business. However, trying to convince them to abandon the central planning and control functions and devolve power to front-line managers is a tough challenge. What will this organization look and feel like? What will be the role of leaders? What will be the impact on the bottom line?

These are not easy questions to answer in advance. We can only look at organizations that have gone down this path and examine their experiences. Ahlsell, Leyland Trucks, and Handelsbanken should provide strong evidence that not only can the system work, but also that the impact on the organization can be stunning. However, in terms of making the change and demonstrating low investment costs and clear short-term benefits, the experience of Leyland Trucks is illuminating.

At Leyland Trucks, various initiatives were tried before the company finally settled on the vision for empowering front-line teams. The total quality program was revived, but it was too procedural and bureaucratic; improvements in MRP II (manufacturing requirements planning) were made in an attempt to reduce production variability, but better programming and scheduling didn't improve productivity; and reengineering was proposed to improve process conformance, but again this didn't engage the workforce and result in the changes expected. In short, none of these initiatives presented a coherent or convincing program for change to hard-bitten employees who had the capability to wreck any new idea that came their way.

As CEO John Oliver noted, "all the radical ideas and initiatives about organizational systems and structures in the world were going to be of no help at all if the underlying propensity to receive change was still negative. None of the eagerness, determination, and urgency of the senior group had conveyed itself to the organization at large."[2] HR director Charlie Poskett was equally dismissive of "technology" and "measurement" approaches. "We thought technology would drive the performance improvements we were seeking," he reflected. "But we soon realized that we had not devoted enough attention to culture. Management change is 30 percent about structure, processes, technology, and measurement, and 70 percent about culture."

The resulting vision was one of empowerment, with the performance management process being changed to allow this process to happen effectively. The actual vision was defined as "empowered people working towards mutually beneficial objectives." The management team brought in an external consultant to act as an independent broker between managers and workers. In other words, he had to be trusted by both groups. One of his first tasks was to survey the opinion of everyone. The results were an eye-opener. The top five issues were (1) job security, (2) mutual trust/honesty, (3) fairness of pay systems, (4) involvement/participation, and (5) management behavior.

Although the top issue was entirely predictable, the others were not. That job security was the unifying purpose at Leyland Trucks was unsurprising given its recent history of downsizing and layoffs. The second issue, however, came as a complete surprise. John Oliver relates his reaction:

> Downstream we discovered this to be a complex need. Not only did the workforce desperately want to trust "those upstairs"; they in turn wanted to be trusted by them. The same need seemed to apply across functions. Perhaps generations exposed to inter-functional strife had led to longstanding enmities across departmental boundaries. People didn't like it, and apparently had a strong desire to trust their colleagues in other areas and in turn to be trusted by them.[3]

The third issue was also surprising. It was not the absolute level of remuneration that rankled people, but the unfairness of the various pay and bonus systems. The fourth and fifth issues, however, really set the scene for what was to follow. The survey showed overwhelming support for the workforce being involved in improving the business. But workers also told senior managers in no uncertain way that *they were the problem.* It was managers' behavior that needed to be changed.

Looking back, Oliver is in no doubt of the benefits:

> We are talking cash, we are talking profitability. This is not some well-intentioned piece of social engineering conjured up by the Human Resources Department. There are numerous and very welcome social spin-offs, but these are tangential. The whole justification for Team Enterprise is that it's the safest, quickest and most cost-effective means of improving your bottom line, long-term and permanently. And don't get hung up on the "long-term." Done correctly, Team Enterprise will start to pay back in months, not years.[4]

Oliver backs up his beliefs with some compelling evidence. In the first two and a half years of the new system, from 1989 to 1991, the company turned in a remarkable performance, with a net profit return on sales of over 10 percent, beating most of its European rivals. In addition, the company reduced operating costs by 24 percent; halved its break-even point from 11,000 to 5,500 trucks per annum; reduced warranty costs by 35 percent and improved build quality; created a more responsive and flexible organization; and achieved a step-change improvement in employee attitudes and satisfaction levels.

Changing Processes Precedes the Devolution of Responsibility: The Order Is Crucial

The main benefits of empowerment are unlikely to be realized until the budget contract has been abandoned and alternative processes put in place. It is the new processes that change actions and behavior.

In some cases leaders have not set out on the beyond budgeting journey with the specific intention of building an empowered organization. It is only when they have made a successful transition to adaptive processes that such an opportunity came into view and within their grasp.

Bjarte Bogsnes believes that although the Borealis model started out as a set of replacement processes using a range of modern management tools, the tools have enabled the firm to devolve responsibility. "New tools such as rolling forecasts and the Balanced Scorecard are not sufficient on their own," he says. "They need a supporting set of leadership principles. The processes and the principles that underpin the performance management model must be clearly aligned with the strategy. Lack of strategic clarity has a knock-on effect down the line."

As Bogsnes notes, one example has been the change from focusing on products to focusing on customers:

> We are an engineering company that makes many products for a variety of markets. We have found it very hard to change mind-sets and to get people to think of customer needs first and products second. It sounds great in theory but is very difficult to apply in practice. Our focus has been on reducing costs, maximizing volume, and speeding up processes. Of course we try to improve customer satisfaction and we have made real progress. Our position in the satisfaction league table has improved significantly in recent years. Much of this improvement can be put down to clearer business unit responsibility for customers. We are also moving toward a better understanding of customer profitability.

Devolving Responsibility:
It Cannot Be "Given," Only "Taken"

According to Oliver, ex-CEO of Leyland Trucks, "management can provide the framework, the infrastructure for empowerment, but it cannot force acceptance on people."[5] This is a telling comment, and its truth can be seen in many of our cases. It takes time for people to realize that senior managers mean what they say. This comes not from statements at seminars and conferences, but from the actions leaders take day after day. It also comes from how people are recognized and rewarded.

Abandoning the budget is one of the most positive actions that leaders can possibly take that says to people "we really mean it." Managers are immediately aware that there is no detailed plan that dictates their actions. They must think for themselves and take responsibility. The learning process is both fast and steep. Managers at all firms we visited told us that they had to understand strategy at both corporate and local levels to be able to carry out their actions. They had to know the principles and boundaries within which they could work. And, most important of all, they had to know that if they made mistakes, they would not be punished.

These changes should not be confused with attempts at "participation" or "empowerment" that were popular in the 1970s. They failed because there was no attempt to change the command-and-control climate. This is about devolving the *responsibility for results*. Ahlsell branch managers, for example, have responsibility for running their own business (the only part they do not control is the selection and procurement of products). Thus, they need a range of skills that were unnecessary in the old system. Building these capabilities takes time. Hiring the right people starts to matter.

With its challenging and responsibility-based work structure, team- and trust-based approach, and relaxed, informal atmosphere, Borealis is a great place to work. It attracts and keeps good, high-quality people. It is no coincidence that Bjarte Bogsnes, the instigator of beyond budgeting at Borealis, switched roles from finance to people management to focus more on the behavioral changes that were needed to support the new approach to performance management. He knew from the beginning that changing mind-sets would be the greatest challenge in rebuilding the organization around a more devolved management approach.

Bogsnes sees this devolution process as a two-way agreement:

> Getting people to respond to stretch targets and provide honest forecasts means that they must trust top management not to question their integrity. We must also trust them with more information to enable them to take the sort of decisions that make this exchange worthwhile. It takes some time to build the self-confidence so essential to this process. It also means having the right people who can accept this challenge. It isn't for everyone. Some people are more comfortable knowing their target and being told what to do to achieve it.
>
> But looking back now we can see even more clearly how this old system was abused. People played the system and learned a

thousand-and-one excuses for nonperformance. The new approach is far tougher. People are exposed. They have to explain what they will do in advance to achieve results and then be prepared to be evaluated against how well they should have done given the circumstances. There is more judgment involved. But it works. Of course a few people try to abuse this system the same way that many people abused the old system. But overall we are pleased with the results.

Overcoming the Resistors: The Forces of Centralization Are Never Far Away

For many managers steeped in the command-and-control culture, devolving responsibility is loosey-goosey, airy-fairy stuff. Their job is to ensure that leaders have control, and that can only be done through hard numbers. They are the self-evident truth, the only basis for sound decisions. This belief finds its ultimate expression in the budget-based performance contract. Macho managers discount any view of organization performance that is not supported by hard numbers.

These people exist in every organization. They are usually a difficult and vocal minority. But, as Tom Johnson noted, those managers who believe that they can determine the ends (results driven by targets and incentives) without attending to the means (how people interact to create results) are lacking an understanding of how success is created and sustained.[6] Jack Welch summed it up neatly when he said that "numbers aren't the vision; numbers are the product. We always say that if you had three measurements to live by, they'd be employee satisfaction, customer satisfaction, and cash flow."[7]

After making many mistakes in the transformation program at Leyland Trucks, Oliver has this advice for dealing with people who fail to understand or support the initiative program:

> Management needs to maximize their attention to the "good guys," that top 80 percent who conform to the idea of positive corporate citizenship. . . . We need to lead by example in marginalizing those who are inherently at odds with both the company and, perhaps, even the world of work. . . . The culture of any organization is

largely created by what we as managers pay attention to, what we care about and what we reward. We may not intend to convey that impression when we devote a disproportionate amount of time with that bottom 20 percent, but we most certainly do.[8]

Many other factions can cause problems for the project team. Wallander discovered that even after finding a receptive audience at the front line, there remained many forces that had to be convinced. Indeed, there was opposition everywhere. He called this the "budget bureaucratic complex." "This complex," he noted, "is made up of all those within companies who feel that their position and their work is coupled to the budget system and that their job and their position might be impaired if the budget system is abandoned. To the complex also belong all the professors, management consultants, and other experts who write books, lecture, and organize conferences about budgeting and its technical complications."

Another way to overcome the resistors is to promote those people who embrace the new values and forge ahead. As Schein points out, the real test is when the new culture creates leaders instead of leaders creating the culture.[9] It is no accident that the most successful cases we studied have had stable executive teams at the top for many years. They have also had chief executives who have been promoted from within and who are well versed in the empowerment philosophy. Conversely, there are some cases in which new chief executives have been parachuted in from outside, with disastrous results for the project.

Letting Go: It's the Ultimate Challenge

The issue of letting go is a tough one for many executive leaders who have spent years climbing the organizational ladder and gaining more power on their ascent. Why should they suddenly give it up? Why should they take the risk? What safeguards do they have that it won't lead to anarchy and loss of control? As then–corporate controller Bjarte Bogsnes recognized at Borealis, it is highly unlikely that the new system will get off the ground unless senior executives are convinced that the new information and control system will be at least as effective as the old one. Peter Senge tells us why: "Giving up control is very difficult, but it's virtually impossible if you have no idea of what you might be getting in its place. . . . See, the big question leaders are asking themselves is, 'What ring am I reaching out to grab as I let go of this other one? Because in between I am hanging in space.'"[10]

Relative improvement contracts and adaptive processes can provide the elusive ring that leaders are reaching for. They fill the void, and, if well thought through, answer all the questions. They provide the framework for a new vision of what the management model might be in three or five years' time. The role of the leader switches from one of planning, coordination, and control to one of inspiring people through a clear vision of change and success. Leaders live the vision day in and day out, spreading the message and inspiring other leaders across the organization. Challenging managerial ambition and stretching performance targets are other important roles of the CEO.

The issue of letting go is influenced by how leaders see their period in office. If they see it as essentially short term with the objective of making immediate gains without considering the long-term survival of the business, then they are less likely to empower front-line people. If, however, they see their time as being devoted to handing on a stronger, more vibrant organization to the next management generation, then they will be more inclined to do so. After thirty years' experience at Handelsbanken, its leaders are still reinforcing and deepening the principles of devolved responsibility.

Changing Recognition and Rewards: It's the Seminal Moment

Some companies have found that the turning point in their switch to a culture of responsibility was when they changed how people were recognized and rewarded.

Changing recognition and rewards was the seminal moment at Groupe Bull and Leyland Trucks, for example. Descarpentries's imaginative formula based on a combination of relative performance measures sent the right signals to all managers at Groupe Bull. They must think and act differently if they are to improve performance. Eradicating a piecework culture at Leyland Trucks that had been ingrained in the assembly plant for decades was an act of courage that said to everyone in the firm that "we really mean it." Other leaders have, like Welch at GE, included an assessment of how managers perform against company values in the annual performance review. This also sends a strong message. At Handelsbanken, the message was different. It said that we are all in this together. Each person depends on and has obligations to others, so we will share the fruits of success evenly across the firm.

Some organizations never went as far as Bull, Leyland, and Handelsbanken. Either they didn't recognize the power and significance of the change, or they hadn't the courage to make it. This is not to say that they didn't make any changes. Clearly they did: Most (but not all) disconnected rewards from fixed performance contracts. But the really successful exemplars appear to have gone much further.

Maintaining the Momentum: It's a Never-Ending Process

In Mårtensson's final letter as CEO to shareholders in 2001, he said that the glue that keeps the organization together is a very strong corporate culture:

> In the new economy, flat network types of organization have become fashionable. Handelsbanken has an advantage here. For several decades we have streamlined this way of working and it has given us major competitive advantages. Our experience is that it takes a very long time to create and to reap all the benefits of this type of organization. It has to be done gradually for the control mechanisms to function correctly and for the organization to mature.[11]

As Mårtensson reminds us, the process of devolving responsibility is continuous. Our case examples tell us that constant reinforcement is necessary to ensure that the changes become the new conventional wisdom and that the new practices get passed down from one managerial generation to the next.

Just to confirm the point, this is what new CEO, Lars Grönstedt, said in the 2002 annual report: "The person who is responsible must be able to compare his or her performance, not with something unreal like a plan or a budget, but with something tangible, such as the result achieved by people of similar responsibilities over the same period of time. That is why benchmarking is such an important instrument for

Handelsbanken, where we have survived perfectly well without budgets for thirty years."[12]

The devolution of responsibility is a gradual process of releasing power and authority, and every opportunity should be taken to deepen it. Today's practitioners should become tomorrow's teachers, and this teaching process should be encouraged at all times.

Few organizations have the right processes and systems in place at the start of the project. IT resources are invariably limited, and choices have to be made to prioritize parts of the implementation process. The project team at Borealis, for example, realized that it couldn't handle everything at once, so it decided to focus on introducing processes and some tools, including the Balanced Scorecard. Bogsnes describes the team's early progress:

> The new tools were quite easy to design. Some we were working on already, like introducing the Balanced Scorecard. The rolling financial forecast is nothing but common sense, and activity accounting is neither new nor radical thinking in Scandinavia. We knew, however, that it would be impossible to design anything to 100 percent, with answers to every possible question that might come up. So we stopped at 80 percent, when we felt confident that the basics made sense. When we jumped, we were fully aware that unforeseen elements would lead to further refinements.

Like Borealis, Ahlsell is a firm that recognizes that building a devolved organization is a long-term project. Even after six years, managers were still refining and developing the systems and progressively giving their people more and more responsibility. As Gunnar Haglund noted, it has been a long process of trial and error. The company made lots of small changes until it got its systems to work the way it wanted them to. These are some examples of the changes that followed the initial implementation:

- Initially the league tables were based only on return on sales. This led to too great a focus on profit at the expense of revenue growth. Therefore, an index of profitability and growth was developed and introduced for business units in the top half of the tables that already achieved an acceptable return.

- Quality was dropped as a separate indicator of performance because it made the system more complex. In practice, profitability and sales growth cannot be achieved without quality being addressed.
- Interest was charged at the accelerated rate of 3 percent per month on slow-moving stock rather than at the general rate of 1 percent used for all other stock.

Abandoning budgeting and embracing the philosophy of empowerment is nothing less than a fundamental change in how businesses are managed; thus, it must be constantly fine-tuned and reinforced. New generations of managers will be seduced by the promise of tighter control, and the gravitational pull of more centralization will be hard to resist—particularly as information technology appears to offer these dubious benefits. However, every executive who truly understands the challenges of the information age will realize that it is the capabilities of people that will separate winners from losers. It takes some time to establish, but, once achieved, it becomes a source of unrelenting competitive advantage.

Chapter Summary

- The main benefits of empowerment are unlikely to be realized until the budget contract has been abandoned and alternative processes put in place. It is the new processes that change actions and behavior.
- Abandoning the budget sends a clear message to all employees about the extent of the change process. It says to people "we really mean it." Managers are immediately aware that there is no detailed plan that dictates their actions. They must either think for themselves and take responsibility or fail to survive.
- There will always be people who block and resist change. However, they need to be proved wrong. Leaders need to spend most of their time with those who support the initiative rather than wasting time trying to convince those who don't.
- Most leaders struggle with the idea that management actions don't need central coordination and control. The role of the leader switches from one of planning actions through plans and budgets to one of inspiring people through a clear vision of change and success.
- Some companies have found that the turning point in their switch to a culture of personal responsibility was when they changed how people were recognized and rewarded, particularly when they included values in the performance appraisal system.
- The process of devolving responsibility is continuous. Our case examples tell us that constant reinforcement is necessary to ensure that the changes become the new conventional wisdom and that the new practices get passed down from one managerial generation to the next. It is a gradual process of releasing power and authority, and every opportunity should be taken to deepen it.

Part IV

Realizing the Full Promise of Beyond Budgeting

Chapter Nine

The Roles of Systems and Tools

Initially these [management information] systems were designed for the needs of the executive team. But several of the organizations went a step further. They created open reporting, making the performance results available to everyone in the organization. Building on the principle that "strategy is everyone's job" they empowered "everyone" by giving each employee the knowledge needed to do his or her job.[1]

—ROBERT KAPLAN AND DAVID NORTON

Kaplan and Norton noted that a number of organizations they examined in the course of preparing their book *The Strategy-Focused Organization* had broken free from the central control model. Despite their detailed methodologies and the opportunity they provided for top-down control, these organizations found the need to open up their reporting systems and empower front-line people. This recognition is at the core of the beyond budgeting vision.

Most of this book has focused on how a number of companies have implemented this vision (some more successfully than others). Those that supported adaptive processes with leadership principles to produce a new coherent model have fared best over the longer term. All cases spent time developing fast and open information systems geared to supporting the decision-making capabilities needed by the front-line manager. Some used recognized tools to provide these capabilities. Others relied more on the ability of people to use their judgment and experience based on the latest available knowledge. For example, although Handelsbanken derives fast information on customer profitability based on the philosophy of activity-based costing, it doesn't use a software package with this label. The bank started with the information required and used its own methodology to provide the solution.

A range of tools has emerged over the past decade designed to solve many of the problems we have explored in this book. Figure 9-1 shows six such tools and how they potentially support the needs of the front-line manager in an adaptive and decentralized organization. As we shall explain, however, the tools are blocked from achieving their potential by the budgeting system.

Shareholder value models align the decisions of internal managers with the expectations and interests of external shareholders. *Benchmarking models* align targets with external or internal best practices and display the results in terms of rankings lists. *Balanced Scorecards* provide a strategic framework for local decisions and provide leading KPIs that tell managers if strategic goals are being met. *Activity-based management*

FIGURE 9-1

How Tools Support the Front-Line Manager

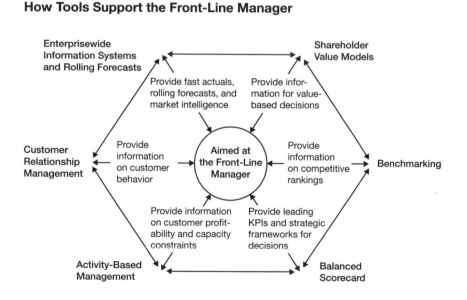

informs managers about the causes of costs and thus better equips them to understand the net profit contributions of products, channels, and customers. *Customer relationship management models* focus managerial actions on knowing and satisfying customer needs profitably. And *enterprisewide information systems and rolling forecasts* join up the disparate functions of the organization and enable managers to relate work and cost inputs to customer outputs across the business. They also enable managers to better anticipate events by providing fast actuals, integrated forecasts, and market intelligence.

Advocates of tools and information systems claim potentially powerful results *if* they are implemented in the right way. They mean that the tools and information systems will work if the culture of the organization is supportive, its leaders are committed, and decision makers have the freedom and capability to act on the information provided. These are big "ifs." The reality is that few tools achieve their objectives. The problem is that although all these tools have been implemented to overcome the systemic failures of the traditional model, the processes that underpinned those failures have been left in place (figure 9-2). Thus it is little wonder that the potential of these tools and models is stymied.

FIGURE 9-2

How the Budgeting Model Undermines the Effectiveness of Tools

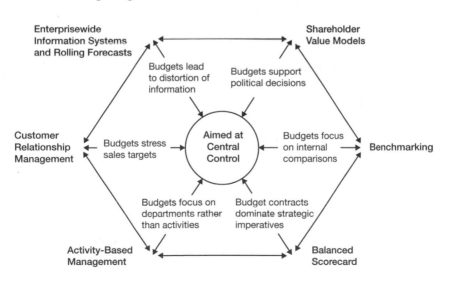

They are, in effect, neutralized by the powerful antibodies of the budgeting immune system.

Budgeting, perhaps more than any other process, defines the cultural norms of an organization. Thus, if any proposed actions threaten those norms, the immune system will spring to their defense. That is why there is often such a chasm between the rhetoric and reality concerning the anticipated results of implementing these tools and systems.

This chapter takes a closer look at each tool and how it can support the adaptive and decentralized organization.

Shareholder Value Models

Aims

Shareholder value models such as economic value added (EVA) and value-based management (VBM) enable managers to make decisions based on creating value greater than the cost of capital. While discounted cash flow (DCF) decision models have been around for decades, they have been used for major project-based decisions rather than for managing the business. EVA and VBM models aim to offer managers an alternative to budget-based management in that they look at every business as a portfolio of assets, products, and customer segments. They then apply resources to them (or terminate existing resources) on the basis of their wealth-creating opportunities.

Understanding key value drivers is central to the shareholder value model. A value driver is any variable that affects the value of the company. Value drivers can be derived from the financial business model and from customer, process, and employee perspectives. To be useful, however, value drivers need to be organized so that managers can identify which have the greatest impact on value and can assign responsibility for them to individuals or teams.

Why Budgets Are Barriers

For these models to work effectively, information needs to be remapped from the vertical flow of a traditional accounting system to the horizontal flow of a value-based information system. This follows the cost stream across the organization until it flows into cost objects such as product lines, customers, market segments, or whole sub-businesses. This assumes an "economic map" of the organization. Only a few companies have successfully embedded these process flows into their mainstream accounting systems. Most are thwarted by the political structure of the organization and the vertical budgeting processes that remain in place to support the hierarchical management information system. Another barrier is the annual focus of the budgeting process. Shareholder value–based decisions are derived from calculating the net present value of future cash flows, yet the decision focus of most managers is on how to meet this quarter's, or this year's, profit target.

Shareholder value–based targets in the hands of "central controllers" are often seen by front-line managers as just another fixed performance contract. Often used under the guise of empowerment ("You can run your own business but you must double shareholder value in three years—or else"), these models offer group finance people ready-made weapons with which to beat operating managers and demand (often impossible) targets without having much understanding of the potential opportunities and problems confronting particular business units.

How They Support Adaptive Processes

Companies aiming at sustainable competitive success can use shareholder value–based targets to set broad guidelines for medium-term business unit goals throughout the organization. Alfred Rappaport, one of the founding fathers of value-based management, believes in the power of shareholder value measures to evaluate and reward executive performance *provided that such measures are based on returns equal to or better than those earned by the company's peer group or by broader market indexes.*[2] Thus, according to Rappaport, it is relative performance that matters: "Fixed priced options reward executives for any increase in the share price—even if the increase is well below that realized by competitors or by the market as a whole."[3]

At the business-unit level, strategy development generally entails identifying alternative options, valuing them, and choosing those with the highest values. Shareholder value models provide a common framework for choosing between these alternative action plans. Judging from the experience of U.K. retailer Boots, shareholder value models can help managers see profitability in ways that traditional accounting numbers cannot. Most Boots' managers believed that the company's prescription drug business was where the real profits were made, only to discover once EVA was applied that nothing could be further from the truth. It was the company's Cinderella operation—the retail stores—that proved to be the outright winner.

How They Support Decentralization

Shareholder value models can support front-line strategy and decision making. Indeed, their real power is that they create a high-performance climate. They challenge ambition and make managers think and act as if they were shareholders and encourage them to take risks in order to grow the business. They also provide a clear decision-making framework. By applying shareholder value criteria, managers can decide between alternative improvement strategies. Such models also enable leaders to see their organizations more as a portfolio of opportunities than as political entities. Moreover, by including the cost of capital in the accounting system, managers are better informed about managing working capital and other assets.

Benchmarking Models

Aims

The philosophy of benchmarking is essentially one of continuous improvement against some world-class standard. Well-chosen benchmarks ensure that firms are measuring performance against best-in-class standards rather than just internally negotiated targets. Benchmarking also gives targets some credibility in the sense that they have been achieved elsewhere.

Why Budgets Are Barriers

Benchmarks set goals that are based on external measures or internal cross-functional comparisons. This goes against the grain of the budgeting process, which aims to set realistic targets that are achievable within the budget year. Thus the extent of underperformance against best-in-class standards loses visibility, and short-term financial targets remain predominant. As the budgetary reporting system gives an illusion of control, the extra effort required to find and collect suitable benchmarks is seldom made. On the other hand, benchmarking in the wrong hands can easily be seen as a big stick with which to beat managers into submitting to impossible targets. This problem is compounded if there is no culture in the organization of measuring success against the competition.

How They Support Adaptive Processes

If used positively, benchmarking models can act as motivational forces for rapid and continuous improvement. Local teams can say to themselves "we can do this," because it has been done elsewhere. Benchmarking snaps them out of the hypnotic effects of the incremental budgeting process. Although there is a risk that benchmarking can lead to "me too" strategies, in the right hands it creates a climate of ambition and achievement. It also provides senior executives with a valuable control. Performance-ranking tables enable them to more fairly evaluate performance, particularly in turbulent times, because doing better than competitors is the real measure of success.

How They Support Decentralization

Benchmarks enable leaders to champion relative success and challenge ambition at every level. Ahlsell is a good example. Monthly performance-league tables are the spur that drive managers forward and constantly test their ability to make step-changes. At higher levels, senior managers can evaluate people against recognized best practices and against their peers. However, great care must be taken to ensure a "like with like" comparison. Sales units at Ahlsell, for example, are measured on return on sales and growth over prior years. Extensive analysis of results has shown that these are truly fair measures of effective local management and that there is no significant correlation of performance with branch size, location, sales product mix, or any other factor.

The Balanced Scorecard

Aims

The Balanced Scorecard was conceived and developed by Robert Kaplan and David Norton in the early 1990s as a response to inadequate performance measurement systems that were primarily geared to reporting financial results against the budget. A well-designed Scorecard should tell the story of a business unit's strategy through a number of cause-and-effect relationships (its "strategy map"). It enables managers to build a "strategy-focused organization." This means setting medium-term goals supported by action plans (invariably cross-functional) that enable these plans to be executed successfully.

Why Budgets Are Barriers

In many organizations where the Scorecard has not been well implemented, it is seen as a few nonfinancial measures attached to a conventional budget. To overcome this problem most companies now attach rewards to the achievement of Scorecard targets for the year ahead. The Scorecard thus becomes a fixed performance contract, just like the budget with all the associated dysfunctional behavior. Even if well designed and well implemented, however, the Scorecard has a tough challenge penetrating the budgeting immune system. The culture underpinning the budget contract is that fixed annual targets must be met; otherwise, negative forces will come into play (e.g., lack of recognition and the loss of reputation and rewards).

The problem is that whereas the Scorecard process drives the company in the direction of medium-term strategic goals supported by cross-functional initiatives, the budgeting process drives the company in the direction of short-term financial goals supported by individual departmental initiatives. Budgets also act as a barrier to the local team's acceptance of responsibility for the Scorecard's success. It is hardly surprising that, despite the Scorecard supposedly determining strategic actions, local managers become cynical when the group finance people keep demanding this quarter's targets.

How It Supports Adaptive Processes

The Scorecard is a tool for helping front-line teams manage strategy. It provides them with a means of ensuring that goals and actions are consistently aligned. It enables targets to be set and reviewed at any time and offers a framework for continuous dialogue between managers and leaders. Rewards can be based on performance in each perspective, provided that relative measures are used rather than fixed numbers to be met by fixed dates. To avoid parochialism, these measures should be dependent on both the team you're in *and* the team you lead.

The Scorecard can also be used to continuously monitor and review strategy. Without the annual focus of the budget, strategy and the essential feedback loops that make that strategy responsive to change are allowed to operate without constraint. A budget-free environment also enables the Scorecard to engage with many more people who were previously denied a voice in the strategy process.

The Scorecard can also be useful for managing projects over an extended period, where targets, measures, and controls need to be more closely monitored. Local managers should review current performance and strategic options in the light of unfolding events and rolling forecasts, and should prepare a number of well-thought-out courses of action to pursue new ideas or react to threats and opportunities. Assumptions and risks inherent in these action plans should be challenged by higher-level managers who need to look at their impact on the business as a whole and ensure that they do not conflict with other projects elsewhere in the company.

How It Supports Decentralization

Kaplan and Norton clearly state that the right approach toward the Scorecard "starts with the recognition that it is not a 'metrics' project; it's a change project." Once the organization is mobilized, they note, the focus shifts to governance, with emphasis on fluid, team-based approaches to deal with the unstructured nature of the transition to a new performance model.[4]

To support the effective devolution of strategy, the Scorecard should engage people at different organizational levels with the strategies and KPIs appropriate to their scope for action and results. In this context it is an educational tool. It helps local managers with little previous experience of strategic management to understand the key issues and learn rapidly.

Ownership of the goals, actions, and indicators attached to the Scorecard should lie at each operating level. Operating managers should have the freedom to change resources used during the year, as long as the agreed-upon KPI parameters are not breached. Scorecards also have a useful role to play in the transition period of moving to a decentralized model. Some senior executives, for example, find it difficult to devolve target setting and need something to approve at the board meeting. The Scorecard can fulfill this requirement.

The Scorecard enables managers at every level to communicate clear goals and the progress being made toward those goals. The Scorecard became a success at Borealis when leaders opened up the information system and posted strategic targets and progress reports on Web sites and on factory and office bulletin boards. Moreover, it became known that even in the boardroom Scorecard reports had at least as much impact as the financial accounts and that management compensation had a significant Scorecard element attached to it. This system is thus open and inclusive and engages everyone in the strategy process and the progress of his or her team or business unit toward achieving strategic goals. This is the major difference between operating the Balanced Scorecard with or without budgets.

Activity-Based Management Models

Aims

Activity-based management (ABM) models enable managers to better understand how activities (pieces of work) add value to products and customers. They are particularly useful when helping managers to identify non-value-adding costs and to estimate the resources needed to support future capacity requirements.

Why Budgets Are Barriers

The problem is that because budgets show the costs of functions and departments (e.g., salaries and buildings) instead of the costs of the activities people perform (e.g., visiting customers and processing orders) managers cannot see the real *cost drivers* of their business. Moreover, it is likely that the budget contains significant amounts of non-value-adding costs (unnecessary work) that remain invisible to managers looking at the financial numbers. The annual budget also tends to fix capacity for the year ahead, undermining the potential of ABM analysis to determine required capacity from a customer demand perspective. ABM practitioners are used to dealing with these problems but their tasks would be made much easier, and their results made more reliable, if these problems were removed.

How They Support Adaptive Processes

ABM models are useful for supporting adaptive management processes because they provide a process and activity focus. Activity-based costs can be used as the basis for benchmarking and to provide operating KPI goals and controls. Activity-based planning models also support rolling forecasts. They are the key to managing costs. For example, ABM helps managers to challenge the value-added content of all process costs and enables them to measure both product- and customer-related profitability. It also highlights excess capacity. This is important in an organization that is responding dynamically to customer demand. By turning the ABM model on its head and starting from anticipated demand, then working back up the resource management chain, ABM enables managers to determine capacity requirements, although estimating resource consumption is a complex issue. This can also be done in conjunction with rolling forecasts of customer demand.

How They Support Decentralization

Front-line people cannot be empowered without relevant information. ABM models can help to solve this problem. Front-line managers need information for value-based decisions, such as whether products, channels, and customers are worthwhile after charging all the costs of supporting them; whether they are achieving cost benchmarks; and whether resources at their disposal add value.

Take front-line employees at Handelsbanken, for example. All branch staff can see the profitability of all transactions as they happen, not weeks afterward when the learning potential has evaporated. Knowing which customer transactions are profitable and unprofitable can have a galvanizing effect on financial results. This does not mean discarding unprofitable customers. The real learning comes from knowing why certain transactions are not profitable and then taking remedial action. Thus, ABM information empowers front-line people, improves their knowledge, and leads to higher profitability. Activity-based management information can also be used to provide front-line people with critical knowledge about the costs of customization and which processes add value (and which should be outsourced or even eliminated).

Customer profitability is a key measure at Handelsbanken because it enables the bank to devolve decision making to front-line managers. The key to producing suitable information for these purposes is that it be realistic and fast. Despite its decentralized organization, there are still significant costs in central departments in Handelsbanken. Attributing these on an activity basis (i.e., based on transactions, wherever possible) enables customer profitability to be measured realistically and online. The information is produced through the bank's ongoing accounting system, which makes reporting extremely fast.

Customer Relationship Management Models

Aims

Customer relationship management models more clearly identify what people need to do not just to satisfy customers, but also to build their loyalty and profitability. The implementation of customer relationship management systems has increased significantly in recent years. Yet, as a recent survey concluded, 70 percent bring negative results.[5]

Why Budgets Are Barriers

The fundamental problem is a misalignment between inside-out planning processes and outside-in customer relationship management strategies. Salespeople are invariably focused on achieving fixed targets based on revenue, product volume, or gross margin, and thus have little interest in whether the firm is meeting customer needs or whether customers are satisfied and profitable. It is perhaps because this inside-out model is so focused on selling products that it is unable to provide managers or salespeople with knowledge about which customer orders are profitable (after charging all the costs they consume). In other words, sales budgets drive the top line but have little or no concern for the bottom line. The result is twofold. First, salespeople aim to satisfy internal targets rather than external customers. And second, it is unlikely that front-line people can be empowered to satisfy customers if, at the same time, the group finance people are demanding that they hit their quarterly sales targets.

How They Support Adaptive Processes

Customer relationship management models are more likely to be effective if they operate with the grain of an outside-in, "anticipate and respond" approach to the market. This relies on the dynamic integration of a number of internal processes that need to combine to provide a seamless solution to the customer. These models focus on responding to customer needs even to the extent of providing customized solutions. With no fixed plans and short-term targets to get in the way, local teams are more likely to accept the responsibility for unit performance based on the *net profitability* of customer outcomes.

How They Support Decentralization

Firms using customer relationship management models reject matrix management structures. Instead, they adopt a principle of customer ownership. Profit centers own customers no matter where transactions take place. Thus teams have total responsibility for customer outcomes.

This encourages a "can do" and "no blame" culture. Managers can do what needs to be done, and fix what needs to be fixed, knowing that there will be someone to support them if it doesn't work out. And managers have focused teams serving and satisfying customers' needs. The result is greater accountability and more satisfied and profitable customers.

Customer relationship management models also provide people with access to the sort of strategic, competitive, and market-based information that was once the preserve of senior executives. These are major culture changes for most marketing and sales teams. They need to get used to building relationships instead of selling products and special deals.

Enterprisewide Information Systems and Rolling Forecasts

Aims

Traditional management information systems mirrored the organizational hierarchy. Information flowed up and down functional lines of control. Enterprisewide information systems and rolling forecasts, however, are designed as though the organization were an interdependent community. The aim is to ensure that everyone has access to the information they need when they need it. It is up to individuals to analyze and interpret that information in any way that serves their purposes.

Why Budgets Are Barriers

Many firms remain fixated on controlling access to this information so that it only reaches those who "need to know." This focus on control has other perverse implications. For example, managers have shown time and again how reluctant they are to provide bad news or honest forecasts if they believe this information will be used against them. Apportioning blame or demanding action from above is rarely the best way to encourage the right response.

Facilitating "drill downs" to minute levels of detail and building information "cockpits" to better enable central control are just some of the features that many information system vendors boast about. This is a serious concern. System designers too often assume that users value the speed and power of data analysis. Hence the notion of the information cockpit, with a few senior executives pulling levers and pressing keys to make decisions that are, more often than not, far better done by front-line managers.

How They Support Adaptive Processes

Local teams need to review strategy at regular intervals. But strategic ideas require hard factual evidence to support their underlying assumptions. And with hundreds of initiatives becoming common in many large companies, common formats and templates are needed to collate and present information. Intranets and Web pages now offer a fast and effective way to deal with these issues. Strategy guidelines, framework models, competitive benchmarks and information, market trends, industry reports, company KPI statements, net present value models, ethical policies, and many other important elements that are needed to formulate strategies can be constantly updated using Web pages. Electronic bulletin boards are another useful tool to enable people to communicate ideas without the need to be in one place at one time.

The information system should be designed to scan and probe for patterns of change in the marketplace. All points of contact with customers and the market in general are tuned to feeding back data into the system. This enables use of data warehousing capabilities and tools to search for patterns of change that are not readily observable in any other way. The system should also support anticipatory management by bridging the time elapsed between lagging and leading indicators. For example, customer acquisitions and defections can be monitored as they happen (at least in industries with regular ordering patterns), strategic initiatives can be monitored as they unfold, and trends can come alive as they appear instantly on the screen.

Rolling forecasts are a key feature of adaptive processes. Organizations such as Borealis and Sight Savers International use rolling forecasts to support their ongoing strategy and resource management decisions. This is a continuous process of reevaluation and prioritization. The capital commitments made in the aggregate project portfolio are compared with rolling forecasts of available capital and then evaluated against those projects in the pipeline. This leads to a more informed decision-making process and one in which projects are always being examined to ensure that they remain strategic and are meeting their performance milestones.

How They Support Decentralization

Enterprisewide information systems and rolling forecasts are more likely to support key decision makers at the front line if these systems are fast, open, and transparent. They will be doubly effective if there are no middle managers filtering or spinning the information with the intention of making it look better than it is.

The information system should be open to all who can benefit from it. It should support insight and collaboration and enable bad news to move around the organization in minutes instead of days, enabling the right people to be working on problems within hours instead of weeks. Bad news must be assimilated quickly and dealt with as a team. Rolling forecasts enable this to happen. But their reliability depends on whether they are prepared and compiled separately from the line management system. Borealis achieves this by looking at forecasts from the perspective of legal entities within the group rather than from the perspective of business divisions. While the line management runs through the division, the legal entity view does not have anyone at its head with line responsibility. So local managers use forecasts for local purposes, and senior executives use forecasts for cash flow and tax planning. The two purposes are different and do not overlap.

Using the Integrative Power of Tools to Support Front-Line People

In many organizations, tools are used by one department or another, but the knowledge provided remains protected within the walls of that department. In adaptive and devolved organizations, this is not the case. The barriers created by the core budgeting process have been removed making the road clear for a more integrated information system to support the needs of front-line people rather than those of the hierarchy. For example:

- Shareholder value models can use critical data supplied by the ABM (rather than the cost budgeting) system to evaluate the worth of product lines, channels, and whole businesses.

- Benchmarks can be used to set medium-term goals within the framework of the Balanced Scorecard. These goals can be based on competitor or peer performance levels and used to display performance within league tables that act as a primary motivator for operating managers. Benchmarks can also use ABM cost-based measures to set medium-term goals.
- The Balanced Scorecard can be used by teams at every level to focus on strategic goals and align these goals with rewards, actions, and key performance indicators. If the chosen value proposition is customer relationship management, for example, then rewards, actions, and KPIs can be aligned accordingly. ABM can be used to eliminate processes and activities that don't provide value for customers. Enterprisewide information systems and rolling forecasts also have a key role to play in making the strategy-focused Scorecard a success. A robust Scorecard depends on constant feedback loops and front-line people who are empowered to act on this information.
- Activity-based management systems are more likely to be useful if they are part of the mainstream accounting system and support front-line decision makers. Knowing which products and customers (and groups of customers) are profitable after charging all the costs of supporting them is perhaps the most important information that can be made available to decision makers.
- Customer relationship management models not only depend on knowing and satisfying customers' needs, but on doing so profitably. ABM information is crucial to the provision of this knowledge, especially if customer-facing people need to make fast decisions concerning integrative solutions involving some customization. Placing customer relationship management models within the framework of the Balanced Scorecard improves the chances of success because the right actions are more likely to be taken to support a customer-focused strategy map.
- Enterprisewide information systems and rolling forecasts are more likely to add value if they are used to support a rich and constantly evolving knowledge-based management system with the Balanced Scorecard at its core.

Beyond budgeting is a leadership philosophy underpinned by a guiding set of principles. To the extent that it is seen as a model, it is a general management model. It is not an information system, nor is it a tool. These already exist. But their problem is that they are all underachieving compared with their potential. One of the main reasons is that their philosophies are out of kilter with the traditional centralized model with budgets. These systems and tools disrupt the existing coherence of the traditional model without establishing a clear alternative.

By following the actions of leaders who have abandoned budgeting, firms can release the full power of these systems and tools. Their role is to support more adaptive management processes and to enable the decentralized organization. But the key to their success is that they should eventually be absorbed within the overall management system.

We have described these tools and models here by their brand names, but in practice these should be transitional identities that will ultimately be lost. The ultimate goal is to build a management model that is *coherent, simple,* and *integrated.* These are the characteristics we observed in the best cases we studied. None of the most mature cases boasted any brand-name tools, yet the philosophies behind them were clearly evident.

- Changes in the external environment are wreaking havoc with traditional control-oriented organizations and their notions of planning and budgeting. In response to these problems, a number of tools have been developed and marketed that purport to solve them. The philosophies behind these tools can only be fully realized in companies that have moved away from the "predict and control" model with budgets to the "adaptive and devolved" model without budgets. Budgets conflict with the aims of these tools and often cause managers to act to achieve their short-term targets at the expense of longer-term value creation. The principles of beyond budgeting release the full power of these tools to support front-line managers and help organizations achieve the new performance management vision.
- Shareholder value models such as EVA and VBM enable managers to make decisions that create value greater than the cost of capital. These models can help firms manage horizontally by answering questions concerning which markets, channels, customers, and products are producing acceptable returns. But their potential is more likely to be realized if leaders abandon the focus on annual numbers and redirect their attention to value creation.
- Benchmarking approaches enable firms to compare their performance with best-in-class results elsewhere as well as with internal peers. Benchmarking models can offer significant potential if leaders are prepared to elevate relative success to the top of the performance agenda.
- The Balanced Scorecard enables all employees to focus on strategy. But it is more likely to reach its full potential if there is no budgeting barrier to act as a counterforce that drives managers toward meeting this year's targets. Nor should fixed performance contracts be established around Scorecard measures.
- Activity-based management enables the creation of multiple profit centers and can lead to radical decentralization with local

managers having the freedom and capability to act with minimal central control and without budgets.

- Customer relationship management models more clearly identify what people need to do not just to satisfy customers, but also to build their loyalty and profitability. These models are in direct confrontation with the "make and sell" business planning model pursued by most firms. To reach the models' potential, firms should switch to an "anticipate and respond" alternative supported by adaptive processes.

- Enterprisewide information systems ensure that everyone receives the information they need when they need it. These systems have the potential to empower front-line people by providing the capabilities they need to make fast decisions. But many leaders are paranoid about opening up the information system to the extent necessary to enable these people to draw their own conclusions and act on them.

- By releasing the full power of these tools and systems, leaders are able to put the "power" into empowerment and enable front-line managers to generate sustained competitive success. They will only do this, however, when the tools have been fully absorbed into a general management model that is *coherent, simple,* and *integrated.*

Chapter Ten

The Vision of a Management Model Fit for the Twenty-First Century

> Change only happens when "creative tension" is created. Creative tension comes from seeing clearly where we want to be, our "vision," and telling the truth about where we are now, our "current reality."[1]
> —PETER SENGE

We began this book by making three main criticisms of the traditional management model. First, its core budgeting process was too protracted and expensive and added insufficient value to its users. Second, it was out of tune with the competitive environment of the information economy. And third, it encouraged dysfunctional and unethical behavior. The problem wasn't just one of inadequate processes, but also one of inappropriate culture.

After spelling out these problems, we went on to show that by replacing the budgeting process with more adaptive processes and devolving more scope and strategic decision making to front-line people, organizations can, over time, overcome these problems. We supported these claims by giving examples of organizations that have transformed their processes and culture. In some cases this has led to stunning success over extended periods of time.

Some have used modern management tools, whereas others have opted for a simplification of the management model and focused on removing bureaucratic blockages and building the spirit of the team. Tools are seen by most organizations as particularly useful in the transition from the old model to the new. In particular, they enable leaders to gradually devolve decisions while maintaining some hands-on controls through the medium of the tools. Tools also fulfill an educational role. For example, managers can learn a great deal about strategy mapping and the alignment of goals, actions, and measures from the Balanced Scorecard. But in the longer term, the objective is to reduce complexity and allow front-line people to use the knowledge at their disposal to make effective decisions.

This final chapter looks at how the new vision of a management model fit for the twenty-first century is achieved by the adaptive and decentralized organization. The achievement of this vision rests on three tests:

1. Is the model simple, low cost, and relevant to its users?
2. Is the model in tune with the success factors of the information economy?
3. Does the model encourage good governance and ethical behavior?

Is the Model Simple, Low Cost, and Relevant to Its Users?

The essence of the adaptive and decentralized management model is that by giving capable and committed people the authority and capability to make fast decisions in their local markets, they will act responsibly, respond appropriately to the threats and opportunities confronting them, and, with one eye on competitive performance, deliver consistent results. Compared with the overbearing bureaucracies of most large companies today (even after "delayering" and reengineering), this is a simple model. It is also a low-cost one, as many beyond budgeting exemplars, such as Handelsbanken, Ahlsell, Borealis, IKEA, and Leyland Trucks, have found.

When we wrote our first case report on Handelsbanken, we described its management model as "advanced." After reading the draft, Wallander called us into his office. "You have misunderstood," he quietly informed us. "The model isn't advanced: *It is simple.*" Then we began to realize what he meant. Organizations used to be smaller, more intimate places where people trusted each other to do what was in the best interests of the business. But over the decades, layers of controls (including budgets) have evolved to make people comply with rigid rules and regulations. These have gradually become more and more intrusive. Examples include directives from the head office on everything from travel allowances to how much can be spent on the Christmas party. The budget is tailor-made for the corporate controller to query every penny that differs from the approved plan. *Simplicity* and *speed* go together in the same way as *budgets* and *controls.* Yet they reflect fundamentally different philosophies of how a business should be managed in the new economy.

The clues to Handelsbanken's exemplary cost performance can be found not in the use of modern management tools (though it used activity-based costing principles long before they were developed elsewhere) but in the management model itself. A flat, simple hierarchy with few controllers; well-trained staff; no budgets to act as barriers to cost reduction; and a few simple-to-understand measures—these are all factors that contribute to maintaining a simple organization and a low cost base. In other words, responsible people with the right information don't need much support.

Budgets absorb huge amounts of time and are very expensive. And though it is obvious, it is worth reminding ourselves that these costs occur every year. Think of your price-earnings multiple. Now take out the costs of the annual budgeting and reporting process. What would be the effect on your market capitalization? A huge figure is the likely answer. Firms such as Borealis and Volvo figure that budgets absorbed up to 20 percent of total management time. Borealis calculated that this time was reduced by up to 90 percent by their elimination. This doesn't mean that hundreds of people are made redundant immediately. But it does mean that the same people have more free time to think about improving their business. In the long run this translates into lower overhead costs and higher profitability.

The new management model is also more relevant to its users. The finance people who were previously under pressure to produce monthly accounts and explain variances are now able to spend more time understanding and supporting the needs of hard-pressed operating managers.

The focus of the model has moved from central to local control. This means that it is the local team that engages in planning and execution. They are the ones in touch with competitive actions and customer needs. And in this model, they are the ones who have the freedom and capability to act.

Leaders also benefit. They have more time to challenge and support front-line people and reinforce principles and boundaries. They are always informed. A fast, transparent information system ensures that there are many checks and balances that provide strong controls.

In hundreds of interviews with leaders and managers at every level in many organizations, we don't recall one person who was unhappy with the new model. No one wanted to return to the old. The only calls for a reversion to the traditional ways were by newly appointed executives who were poorly briefed by the boards that recruited them.

Is the Model in Tune with the Success Factors of the Information Economy?

Chapter 1 outlined a number of key changes in the business environment that have forced leaders to focus on a range of new competitive imperatives, which will determine success or failure in the information economy. Figure 10-1 shows the relationship between these success factors and the adaptive and decentralized organization. Sustainable, competitive success and value creation is driven by four direct value drivers: innovative strategies, low costs, loyal and profitable customers, and ethical reporting. However, these drivers will be ineffective unless front-line people have the scope and knowledge to maximize their power. This scope and knowledge is supplied by adaptive processes (supported by tools as appropriate). And the effectiveness of adaptive processes and tools is reinforced by the leadership principles that govern the decentralized organization.

Because the last factor (good governance and ethical reporting) is also our third "vision" test, we cover it separately in the next section. This section examines the first five success factors, looking at each and spelling out why the budgeting model fails to support it and then how the principles of the adaptive and decentralized organization *do* support it.

FIGURE 10 - 1

How the Beyond Budgeting Management Model Supports the New Success Factors of the Information Economy

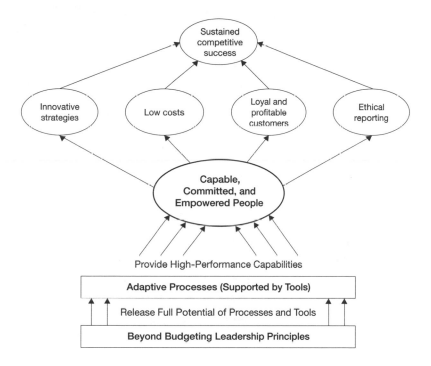

Sustainable Competitive Success and Value Creation

In their frantic efforts to satisfy shareholders, some firms set higher and higher stretch targets as the way to maintain quarterly profits. But this only goes so far because managers eventually run out of efficiency and cost-cutting options. The result, more often than not, is a profit graph that looks more like a roller coaster than a steady upward curve as firms expand to meet aggressive targets only to cut back when they become impossible. But shareholders don't want gyrating profit graphs. They want consistent, sustainable performance that is better than that of competitors (relative performance is neutral to all market conditions). This requires the alignment of strategic decisions with long-term wealth creation and a measurement and reward focus on beating the competition rather than some negotiated number.

Leaders in adaptive and decentralized organizations focus their attention (either explicitly or implicitly) on creating wealth over the longer term. In particular, they focus on setting high performance expectations and stretching people's ambitions. This is done by setting aspirational goals based on a range of competitive criteria and then providing managers with the freedom and capabilities to achieve them. Those companies that have adopted these principles have proceeded to beat the competition. In particular, Handelsbanken, Ahlsell, and IKEA have been head and shoulders above their sector peers for many years.

Find and Keep the Best People

In a McKinsey survey of thousands of managers worldwide, it was clear that they valued freedom, autonomy, and challenge much more than pay and rewards (they could obtain this latter satisfaction almost anywhere).[2] Thus, it is hardly surprising that good managers gravitate to those firms that have flat, devolved management structures and that offer them the chance to "run their own business" while providing all the benefits of a large organization.

Hierarchical structures that are governed by financial budgets offer ambitious managers limited scope for challenge, opportunity, and personal development. Nor are they designed for entrepreneurial activity and risk taking. They are designed for control. Similarly, the budgeting process is not conducive to acquiring key people when they are available. Indeed, talented people are not always around when they are needed. So when they signal their availability, they need to be snapped up. But the budgeting model can act as a real barrier by preventing required action.

Adaptive and decentralized organizations attract talented people by providing a culture of responsibility within which they have the freedom and capability to make decisions. Empowerment is important. So is a leadership style that creates a climate of challenge and ambition. But neither of these two elements will be effective unless the firm creates sufficient positions of responsibility that enable people to use their knowledge to deliver exceptional customer value and produce results that consistently beat the competition.

Both Ahlsell and Handelsbanken have addressed this problem by creating hundreds of profit centers. These provide ambitious managers with the opportunities they crave. The firms are also careful to recruit and develop people who can operate within such a high-responsibility environment. This is a real competitive advantage, and it is a virtuous circle. The challenge and pace of their development make it difficult for such people to return to a more standard hierarchical organization.

Continuous Innovation

Despite the launch of radically new business models in every market sector, many firms still maintain that product innovation is the province of the R&D department and that strategy innovation is the province of senior planners. But bloated bureaucracies and budgetary controls are the enemies of insight and innovation. They stifle creativity ("grinding genius into gruel," as one article put it[3]) through a rigid system of budgetary controls that fail to provide the right management climate within which creative people can thrive.

The adaptive and decentralized model challenges this approach. Managers are more likely to think and act imaginatively without a fixed performance contract hanging over their heads. Instead of haggling over budget-based numbers, managers are forced to think more imaginatively about how they can achieve double-digit growth. Eradicating the budgeting mentality also opens the way for the effective sharing of knowledge and best practices across the company as the protective barriers erected by the budgeting process are dismantled.

Firms like Handelsbanken, Ahlsell, and Bulmers encourage innovative thinking at all levels of the business and ensure that all those who can contribute to strategy do so. Rather than focusing on how to do the same things better, their managers are constantly challenging current business concepts and looking for new ways of delivering exceptional customer value.

Low Costs

To combat falling prices and margins, most companies aim to become "lean and mean" by flattening hierarchies, reengineering processes, reducing fixed costs, and improving efficiency—which usually means doing the same amount of work with fewer people. The problem is that cost-reduction initiatives driven from the top down through the hierarchy are rarely as effective as adopting a devolved management model within which self-managed teams are motivated to relentlessly identify and eliminate unnecessary work. The issue is one of ownership. In the traditional model, ownership of the problem lies with the hierarchy, whereas in the devolved model it lies with the front line.

As a result, adaptive and decentralized organizations have lower costs. Operating managers challenge resources used rather than seeing them as entitlements. Handelsbanken has the lowest cost-to-income ratio of any bank in Europe. One reason is that there are no budgets to lock in costs. In their place there are highly visible relative KPIs (e.g., cost-to-income ratios) for each self-managed team. These place responsibility on all employees to look for ways to reduce them and thus improve their key profitability measures (and their profit share).

As Wallander recognized at an early stage, the best opportunities for cost reduction lie in adopting a flat management structure that enables front-line employees to respond quickly to customer requests. The annual negotiation of departmental budgets works against the grain of this approach. Resources are allocated centrally, and costs are seen as entitlements and are hard-wired into the fabric of the business structure.

By replacing the dependency culture with one based on personal responsibility, leaders shift the burden of performance improvement from the top to the middle, and often to the bottom, of the organization. Ahlsell's Gunnar Haglund described it as moving from "push" to "pull," and at Handelsbanken they say that "The competitive system drives itself."

Profitable and Loyal Customers

Knowing customers' exact needs is not often included on the agenda of most sales planning meetings. Sales budgets tend to be constructed and monitored on the basis of segmenting customers by product group, size, lifestyle, or some other grouping that reflects ways of targeting customers without listening to their particular needs. Under this "inside-out" approach, managers believe that customers can be satisfied by improving the product or service.

Adaptive and decentralized organizations know how customers want to conduct business with them. Key issues are whether customers just want the lowest-cost transaction, added-value services, or customized solutions. Under this "outside-in" approach, firms know how to satisfy these requirements. They listen to their customers and design their operating processes to specifically address their needs.

Fast response to customer requests is also important. Thus, people at the front line must have the authority to make quick decisions. But these decisions must also be profitable. Thus, measuring order-line profitability is crucial. Handelsbanken managers know about profitable customers. They have online customer profitability information and know each customer's particular needs.

Does the Model Encourage Good Governance and Ethical Behavior?

It is clear that following the spate of corporate governance scandals in 2001–2002, people have had enough of quick fixes, cheating, manipulation, and the greed that seems to be an accepted part of everyday life inside many organizations today. They want to work in a more virtuous organization. They want to have a better balance between work and personal life, to trust people, to be part of a team. They want to be reconnected with their leaders. They want to know what the company stands for and where it is going. They want to play their part in its journey and share in its success. And, most important of all, they want to find more meaning in their working lives.

Yet few organizations today can offer such prospects. Instead, success is seen in terms of an aggressive fixed performance contract that must be met at all costs. Such a contract discourages virtuous behavior. It assumes that people act as "rational" economic beings who will only work hard if sufficient financial incentives are dangled in front of their noses. It plays on people's fears—the fear of losing bonuses, the fear of losing promotions, and the fear of losing their reputations and, ultimately, their jobs. It pits team against team in the annual dog fight for resources and favors from the head office. Few people enjoy that sort of management climate.

However, it takes both a procedural and cultural transformation to achieve the sort of ethical changes required. Adaptive and decentralized companies have a better chance of achieving this balance. They are, by and large, *virtuous organizations*. They are held together by strong values and inviolate principles. The frenetic quarterly scramble to reach the numbers has been eliminated, along with all the concomitant overtime and stress. But, as we have seen, beyond budgeting is not a soft option. It exposes nonperformers. It challenges people all the time. You can't just agree on a number. You have to show people that you can actually achieve real performance improvements, and must always be prepared to be judged against others with similar problems and opportunities.

Openness, transparency, and accountability are the keys. As we noted in chapter 6, Handelsbanken and Ahlsell have developed a number of important principles and practices that underpin these values. These principles explain much about how they promote good governance and ethical behavior. Fudging the numbers is not an issue. There is transparency everywhere. There is no fixed performance contract to encourage gaming. There is no profit taking across the company that encourages false margins that are unrelated to real customers. There are no middlemen treating the information or giving it some particular spin. And there is complete openness of information. It is unlikely that anyone can make major errors or fudge the numbers and not be seen.

Reconnecting Front-Line People to the Organization

Fraud or corruption is much more likely to occur in organizations where people are disconnected from leaders, feel no responsibility for their actions, and see greed and manipulation at the top as a license to act with the utmost self-interest. The problem is that this disconnection is an increasing feature of many large organizations. Strategy expert Gary Hamel believes that "the number one problem in America today is that we have a work force that has had to pay a disproportionate price for the strategic mistakes of top management. And the challenge is how do you reconnect these people emotionally and intellectually to the company."[4]

How can employees be reconnected with executive leaders and vice versa? What doesn't work is just talk, or even management seminars. We believe that the adaptive and decentralized management model can provide many of the answers. People at every level feel involved. They are connected to their leaders. They are free to express opinions and suggest new ideas for improvement. They are in control of their work. They are emotionally committed. They generally look forward to going to work. And they are open and honest with each other.

Adaptive processes (underpinned by relative improvement contracts) and a radically decentralized organization (underpinned by the devolution of responsibility to front-line people), when fused together, offer organizations a coherent alternative to the traditional budgeting model. Moreover, by giving front-line people more of a strategic voice, such a structure enables them to be reconnected to the organization's purpose and its strategic goals.

Margaret Wheatley, author of *Leadership and the New Science,* gives a startling example of how this alternative model has been applied by the U.S. Army and Marines:

> Both the Army and the Marines now have the technology to provide every individual soldier with information about what's occurring on the battlefield, information that formerly was known only by the commanders. Through extensive field tests, the Army has discovered that when individuals have such information and know how to interpret it because they know the "commander's intent," they can make decisions that lead to greater success in battle.[5]

This is the new world of the front-line manager, not only in the military, but also in business organizations. The benefits of trusting people and harnessing all their energy and imagination far outweigh the inherent risks.

In searching for a better way forward, it is sometimes instructive to look back to how earlier organizations functioned before the measurement industry began to dominate organizational life. The Quakers in both the United Kingdom and in the United States were few in number but created the lion's share of wealth in both countries during the late eighteenth century. In Philadelphia in 1769 (then the United States' largest city), more than three-quarters of the wealthy elite had Quaker backgrounds, even though the group only represented one-seventh of the population. Likewise in the United Kingdom, the Quakers founded businesses in iron founding, finance, chemicals, and confectionery.[6]

What was it that created so much success? The Protestant work ethic and religious zeal had much to do with it, but how they organized their businesses was the secret. The Quakers had a unified belief system, they watched each other's moral progress, and they founded schools for their children. They supported their fellows generously in trouble and spent time in each other's company, forming business partnerships that were often cemented in marriage. In modern management parlance, they were great networkers, but it was not networking born out of the desire to exploit each other's usefulness. There was a strong vein of mutuality and self-help that made virtues of trust and fairness in their affairs.[7] They had much in common with today's "learning organizations." They trusted each other because they had a common set of beliefs and values. Profit was a means to an end rather than being the sole purpose of the business. It was used to renew the enterprise by reinvesting in its productive capacity. Their leaders also had a "legacy mentality." They wanted to build something that would stand the test of time, as indeed most of their organizations did. There are some organizations that still operate this way (e.g., in the nonprofit sector). But this model is a long way from where most organizations are today—ruled by short-term fixed performance contracts and remotely controlled by financial numbers.

Eighteenth-century Quakers achieved a symbiotic relationship between personal responsibility and performance measures. Measurement wasn't a form of remote control. It was a feature of self-regulation. How do we recapture the virtues of common purpose and mutuality so apparent in Quaker organizations and still to be seen in the nonprofit sector today? And how can we apply them to modern complex organizations?

We believe that the vision of a new adaptive and decentralized management model presented in this book is the answer. It is based on releasing the enterprise, energy, and capabilities of large numbers of people supported by adaptive processes, appropriate tools, and clear leadership principles. There is no place for fixed performance contracts and remote-control management. Leaders need to place more faith, responsibility, and trust in their operating people. The result will be a management model that offers a unique source of competitive advantage. It can be observed, even described, but it is very difficult to copy.

Chapter Summary

- The new vision of a management model fit for the twenty-first century can be achieved by the adaptive and decentralized organization. Its fitness rests on three tests:
  1. Is the model simple, low cost, and relevant to its users?
  2. Is the model in tune with the success factors of the information economy?
  3. Does the model encourage good governance and ethical behavior?
- By any standards, the adaptive and decentralized management model is simple, low cost, and relevant. The protracted annual cycle of preparing and negotiating budgets has disappeared. Because performance responsibility has been transferred to front-line people, there is no need for layers of controllers. There is far less bureaucracy, and the protectionist mind-set of the cost budgeting process has been cast aside. Users are also happy. They find that finance people have more time for them. And they are the beneficiaries of a fast, open information system primarily geared to their needs.
- The new model is more in tune with the information economy. Its processes and leadership culture champion sustained competitive success. Its culture of responsibility and focus on developing front-line managers are attractive, especially to new recruits who can pick and choose who they join. It has removed the top-down controls that stifle innovation. Employees at every level assume responsibility for rooting out unnecessary costs. And this model enables people to listen to customers (both internal and external) and focus on profitable customer outcomes.
- The new model also promotes good governance and ethical behavior. The primary driver of unethical behavior (the fixed performance contract) has been removed. In its place there is a relative improvement contract that operates in a climate of openness, transparency, and accountability.

Glossary

ACCOUNTABILITY: The outputs that a work unit is expected to produce, and the performance standards that managers and employees of that unit are expected to meet.

ACTION PLANS: Business unit initiatives geared toward improving performance against an agreed-upon goal or strategic objective.

ACTIVITY: A unit of work, or task, with a specific output. Activities are distinct, normally are steps in a process, and are capable of being flow-charted and measured. Examples of activities are processing an order and issuing a check.

ACTIVITY COST DRIVER: A unit of measurement for the level (or quantity) of the activity performed.

ACTIVITY-BASED COSTING: Under activity-based costing, costs are analyzed by applying them to activities (or pieces of work, such as processing an order) rather than general ledger accounts (e.g., salaries) that tell little about the drivers (i.e., causes) of costs. Activity costs are then traced to cost objects (e.g., a branch or set of customers) in accordance with how the activities are actually consumed (e.g., how many orders were processed by a central department for a branch). This is done by identifying output measures (e.g., the number of orders processed) and unit costs (e.g., $10 per order).

ACTIVITY-BASED MANAGEMENT (ABM): The management processes that use the information provided by an activity-based cost analysis to improve organizational profitability. The overall aim of ABM is to cut across the functional hierarchical view of costs, align work and resource consumption with customer value, and manage the business through its processes. The goal of ABM is to enable customer needs to be satisfied while making fewer demands on organizational resources.

ADAPTIVE AND DECENTRALIZED ORGANIZATION: An organization that operates with adaptive management processes and that devolves performance responsibility to front-line people close to the customer.

ADAPTIVE MANAGEMENT PROCESS: A process of planning and decision making that is not tied to a specific plan or budget. Operating managers and teams have significant local discretion to use their knowledge and judgment to make decisions that are congruent with the organization's purpose and strategy.

ANTICIPATE-AND-RESPOND: A description of a business that takes an "outside-in" view of business planning, first anticipating what customers will need and then responding to that need by acquiring the resources necessary to satisfy it.

ASPIRATIONAL GOALS: Goals that are set based on significant step-changes in performance and that are likely to be reached only with exceptional changes in performance over a number of years.

BALANCED SCORECARD: A strategic management and measurement framework that views a business unit's performance from four perspectives: financial, customer, internal business process, and learning and growth. It enables managers to map and describe a business unit's strategy, and review its progress periodically.

BENCHMARKING: The process of studying and comparing how other organizations perform similar activities and processes. These organizations can be either internal or external to the firm and are selected because they are known to have excellent performance for the benchmarked process or result.

BEYOND BUDGETING: A set of guiding principles that, if followed, will enable an organization to manage its performance and decentralize its decision-making process without the need for traditional budgets. Its purpose is to enable the organization to meet the success factors of the information economy (e.g., being adaptive in unpredictable conditions).

BUDGET: A plan expressed in financial terms, a basis for controlling performance, an allocation of resources, an entitlement to spend, and a commitment to a financial outcome.

BUDGET CONTRACT: A commitment resulting from the delegation of accountability for achieving agreed-upon outcomes to a divisional, functional, or departmental manager.

BUDGET GAMES: Attempts by managers to manipulate information and targets and take non-value adding actions to achieve their budgets and to attain high bonuses.

BUDGETING PROCESS: The practice of preparing, submitting, and agreeing upon a budget between one organizational level and another.

CAPABILITY TO ACT: The capabilities that people have to execute their decisions. This includes the resources, tools, training, and information at their disposal, and the removal of bureaucratic constraints.

CAPACITY CONSTRAINTS: Limitations on the quantity that can be produced because the capacity committed for some activity resources (e.g., plant space or number of machines) cannot be changed in the short run.

CENTRAL CONTROL: The control exercised by senior executives over decisions taken by managers in divisions and business units to ensure that their actions conform with group policies, plans, and directives.

CONTINUOUS IMPROVEMENT: An approach to performance management that aims to continuously improve against benchmarks or competitors.

COORDINATION: The linking of commitments between one part of an organization and another to satisfy the needs of external customers.

COST CENTERS: Responsibility centers whose managers and other employees control costs but not revenues or investment levels.

COST OF CAPITAL: The return that the organization must earn on its investments in order to meet the requirements of its investors. This is the interest rate that organizations use in their time value of money, discounting, or compounding, calculations.

CUSTOMER ACCOUNTABILITY: The emphasis placed on individuals being accountable for satisfying customers' needs both internally and externally.

CUSTOMER PROFITABILITY: The *net profitability* of individual customers or groups of customers (e.g., channels and market segments) after assigning income and all the costs consumed (e.g., production, marketing, selling, distribution, and administration).

CUSTOMER RELATIONSHIP MANAGEMENT (CRM): The process of knowing and satisfying customer needs profitably.

CUSTOMER VALUE PROPOSITION: The unique set of promises (e.g., price, quality, product features, and service convenience) that defines the company in the eyes of the customer.

DECENTRALIZATION: The devolution of decision-making responsibility from the corporate center to divisions and business units. *Radical decentralization* delegates *performance* responsibility to managers and teams at (or near) the front line.

DEVOLUTION: The act of transferring performance responsibility from the center to operating and front-line managers and teams without defining this responsibility in terms of a specific plan or budget.

ECONOMIC VALUE ADDED (EVA): An evaluation of a business unit or product line's financial desirability using its residual income. EVA is defined as the (adjusted) after-tax profit for the period less the (weighted average) cost of capital. Thus, if a company has after-tax profits of $20 million, shareholder funds of $100 million (with a cost of capital of 12 percent), and borrowings of $50 million (with a net of tax interest cost of 4 percent), its EVA would be $6 million (profit of $20 million less equity cost of $12 million and debt cost of $2 million).

EMPOWERMENT: The act of providing employees who are closest to operating processes, customers, and suppliers with the freedom and capability to make decisions that are consistent with the company's strategy and values.

ENTERPRISEWIDE INFORMATION SYSTEMS: Computer-based management information systems that connect every part of an organization and provide information to those who need it when they need it.

ETHICAL INFORMATION: Information that is transparent and untreated by managers in an effort to make it look better than it really is.

FAST AND OPEN INFORMATION: Relevant information that can be accessed by individuals when required from an organization-wide data repository and interpreted in any way that supports their decision-making requirements.

FIXED PERFORMANCE CONTRACT: The outcome of a process of agreeing upon targets, incentives, plans, resources, cross-company commitments, and performance measures between a superior and subordinate for a specified period. Its terms and conditions can either be explicit (usually a written letter between the parties) or implicit (custom and practice tell the parties what the likely outcomes will be). In addition to the six elements just identified, the terms of such a contract are likely to include a time period within which targets must be achieved, the limits of authority, and the reporting intervals.

FIXED TARGET: A financial or nonfinancial target that is represented by a fixed number to be achieved within a specified period of time (e.g., an annual budget or Balanced Scorecard KPI target).

FORECAST: A periodic financial statement of the most likely outcome of income and expenditure related to a business or project for a specified period of time. Forecasts are often used to evaluate whether the current year is on track to achieve the approved budget. A forecast may also be made for a nonfinancial measure.

FREEDOM TO DECIDE: See empowerment.

GOVERNANCE: The framework of principles, values, boundaries, and control systems that is defined for managing empowered actions.

INCENTIVE COMPENSATION: The linking of rewards agreed upon in advance to the achievement of fixed targets within a specified period of time.

INTELLECTUAL ASSETS: There are three types of intellectual assets: Human capital or competencies include the experience, skills, and capabilities of people. Structural or internal capital includes patents, trade marks, and copyright; the store of knowledge in databases and customer lists; and the design and capability of information systems. Finally, market-based or external capital includes the profitability and loyalty of customers and the strength of brands, licenses, and franchises.

INTERNAL MARKET: The simulation of an external market between buyers and sellers but operated inside an integrated organization. Thus, internal service providers become suppliers to operating unit customers. Prices are negotiated and service levels agreed upon.

KEY PERFORMANCE INDICATORS (KPIs): Performance measures used to set goals and assess an organization's performance based on its critical success factors.

KEY VALUE DRIVERS: Those elements, such as quality, time, cost reduction, innovativeness, customer service, or product performance, that create long-term profitability for the organization.

KNOWLEDGE MANAGEMENT: A process that makes the most effective use of the intellectual capital of a business. Its purpose is to enable people across a large organization to share information and insights that lead to performance improvement.

MAKE-AND-SELL: A description of a business that takes an "inside-out" view of business planning, first planning what to make and sell and then persuading customers to buy its output.

NET PRESENT VALUE (NPV): The summation of the current value of a stream of future net cash flows after adjusting for the time value of money.

NON-VALUE-ADDED ACTIVITY: An activity that presents the opportunity for cost reduction without reducing the product or service value potential to the customer.

OPERATING BUDGET: A forecast of revenues and expenses based on a plan that has been agreed upon by management as the target for the next operating period (typically one year). The operating budget also authorizes spending on discretionary activities, such as research and development, advertising, maintenance, and employee training, and is the basis against which such expenditure is controlled.

OPERATING MANAGEMENT CYCLE: A cycle of operating management reviews during which day-to-day operating issues are addressed.

PERFORMANCE MANAGEMENT MODEL: The whole process of setting goals and rewards, deciding strategies and action plans, managing resources, coordinating activities, and measuring and controlling performance for an organization.

PERFORMANCE RANKINGS (LEAGUE TABLES): The comparison of performance outcomes between a company and its subunits with their peer groups. The position in the league table can act as a spur to higher levels of achievement.

PROCESS: A specific ordering of work activities across time and place, with a beginning, an end, and clearly identified inputs and outputs, and in which resources are consumed.

PROFIT CENTER: A responsibility center whose employees control revenues and costs but not the level of investment.

RADICAL DECENTRALIZATION: The devolution of performance responsibility to managers and teams at (or near) the front line.

RELATIVE IMPROVEMENT CONTRACT: An implicit agreement between a superior and subordinate to use their best endeavors to continuously improve performance against specified benchmarks, peers, competitors, or prior years. Performance is evaluated with the benefit of hindsight.

RESPONSIBILITY CENTER: An organizational unit for which a manager is accountable in the form of cost (a cost center), revenue (a revenue center), profits (a profit center), or return on investment (an investment center).

ROLLING FORECAST: A financial forecast (usually including a few high-level figures such as sales, costs, and cash flows) that is updated on a rolling basis. A typical rolling forecast would be prepared each quarter to cover the following five quarters. It is not tied to a particular fiscal year-end review but enables managers to continuously review strategy and cash requirements.

ROLLING REVIEW CYCLES: The process of reviewing performance that is not tied to a particular fiscal year. Typical review cycles are annual (looking two to five years ahead) and quarterly (looking five to eight quarters ahead).

SHAREHOLDER VALUE MODELS: Models such as EVA (economic value added) and VBM (value-based management) that enable managers to make decisions on the basis of their impact on shareholders' wealth.

STRATEGIC CONTROL: The process of providing information about the competitive performance of the overall business unit, both financially and in meeting customers' needs, for control purposes.

STRATEGIC INFORMATION: Information that guides the long-term decision making of the organization. Strategic information can include the profitability of products, services, and customers; competitor behavior and performance; customer preferences and trends; market opportunities and threats; and technological innovations.

STRATEGIC MANAGEMENT CYCLE: A cycle of strategic management reviews during which major strategic issues are addressed.

STRETCH TARGETS: Those targets that represent significant increases in the targeted amount or goal above the existing targets or goals, and is more than an incremental improvement over current performance.

TOTAL SHAREHOLDER RETURN: The sum of gross dividends plus the increase in share value expressed as an annual compound rate of growth (of the original share acquisition cost) between two points in time.

TRANSFER PRICE: An internally set transaction price to account for the transfer of goods and services between different parts of the same firm.

VALUE CHAIN: A sequence of activities whose objective is to provide a product to a customer or to provide an intermediate good or service in a larger value chain.

VALUE-ADDED ACTIVITY: An activity that, if eliminated in the long run, would reduce the product's service to the customer.

VALUE-BASED MANAGEMENT (VBM): A decision-support process that combines historic and predictive views with financial and nonfinancial drivers of the business. It enables managers to evaluate alternative plans by measuring their impact on (future) free cash flows and thus, by applying an appropriate cost of capital discount rate, on shareholder value today.

VARIANCE ANALYSIS: The decomposition of differences between actual and estimated costs into amounts related to specific factors causing the variance between actual and estimated costs.

WORK UNIT: A grouping of individuals who utilize the firm's resources and are accountable for performance.

ZERO-BASE BUDGETING: An approach to agreeing on discretionary expenditures that assumes that the starting point for each item of discretionary expenditure is zero, and involves a process of ranking expenditure options.

Notes

Introduction

1. Price Waterhouse Financial and Cost Management Team, *CFO: Architect of the Corporation's Future* (New York: Wiley, 1997), 84.

2. Marshall Loeb, "Jack Welch Lets Fly On Budgets, Bonuses, and Buddy Boards," *Fortune,* 29 May 1995, 73.

3. Robert Simons, *Levers of Control* (Boston: Harvard Business School Press, 1995), 83.

Chapter One

1. Peter Drucker, "Planning for Uncertainty," *The Wall Street Journal,* 22 July 1992.

2. Russ Banham, "Revolution in Planning," *CFO,* August 1999, <http://www .cfo.com/article/1,5309,1237|M|303,00.htm>, (accessed 11 March 2001).

3. Ram Charan and Geoffrey Colvin, "Why CEO's Fail," *Fortune,* 21 June 1999, 31–40.

4. Economist Intelligence Unit Ltd., "Beyond Budgets," *Business Europe* 40, no. 9 (2000), quoted in Andy Neely, Michael R. Sutcliff, Herman R. Heyns, et al., *Driving Value through Strategic Planning and Budgeting—A Research Report from Cranfield School of Management and Accenture* (Accenture, 2001), 4.

5. Anthony Atkinson, Rajiv D. Banker, Robert S. Kaplan, and S. Mark Young, *Management Accounting,* 2d ed. (Upper Saddle River, NJ: Prentice-Hall International, 1997), 724.

6. Hackett Benchmarking Solutions, <http://www.thgi.com/pprfax.htm>, (accessed 14 April 2002).

7. Fran Littlewood, "Look Beyond the Budget," *The London Times,* 11 January 2000.

8. Neely et al., *Driving Value,* 4.

9. Hackett Benchmarking Solutions.

10. Answerthink, "Corporate Strategic Planning Suffers from Inefficiencies, Study Reveals," 11 October 1999, <http://www.answerthink.com/news_and_events/ press_release_1999_detail.asp?ident=13>, (accessed 14 April 2002).

11. Answerthink, "Nearly Half of Companies Unprepared to Foresee and Deal with Sudden, Non-Financial Types of Risk, Study Concludes," 20 March 2002, <http://www.answerthink.com/news_and_events/press_release_2002_detail.asp?id ent=234>, (accessed 14 April 2002).

12. Keith A. Russell, Gary H. Siegel, and C. S. Kulesza, "Counting More, Counting Less," *Strategic Finance,* September 1999, <http://www.mamag.com/strategicfinance/1999/09g.htm>, (accessed 7 October 1999).

13. Stephan Haeckel, *Adaptive Enterprise* (Boston: Harvard Business School Press, 1999), 39.

14. Answerthink, "Nearly Half of Companies Unprepared."

15. H. Thomas Johnson, *Relevance Regained* (New York: The Free Press, 1992), 22.

16. Johnson, *Relevance Regained,* 23.

17. Carol J. Loomis, "The 15% Delusion," *Fortune,* 5 February 2001, 52–53.

18. Stephanie Kirchgaessner and Richard Waters, "WorldCom's Whiz-kid," *Financial Times,* 29 June 2002, 13.

19. Robert Simons, *Levers of Control* (Boston: Harvard Business School Press, 1995), 83.

20. Cathy Lazere, "Altogether Now," *CFO,* February 1998, 29.

21. Answerthink, "Nearly Half of Companies Unprepared."

Chapter Two

1. Marshall Loeb, "Jack Welch Lets Fly On Budgets, Bonuses, and Buddy Boards," *Fortune,* 29 May 1995, 73.

2. PR Newswire, "Corporate Strategic Planning Suffers from Inefficiencies," *PR Newswire,* 25 October 1999.

3. Robert S. Kaplan and David P. Norton, *The Strategy-Focused Organization* (Boston: Harvard Business School Press, 2001), 274.

4. Gary Hamel, "Bringing Silicon Valley Inside," *Harvard Business Review,* September–October 1999, 76.

5. Kaplan and Norton, *Strategy-Focused Organization,* 274.

6. Answerthink, "Nearly Half of Companies Unprepared to Foresee and Deal with Sudden, Non-Financial Types of Risk, Study Concludes," 20 March 2002, <http://www.answerthink.com/news_and_events/press_release_2002_detail.asp?ident =234>, (accessed 14 April 2002).

7. Chris Argyris, "Empowerment: The Emperor's New Clothes," *Harvard Business Review,* May–June 1998, 100.

8. Watson Wyatt Worldwide, "Human Capital Index: Linking Human Capital and Shareholder Value," January 1999, <http://www.watsonwyatt.com/research/resrender.asp?id=W-292&page=1>, (accessed March 11, 2001).

9. Elizabeth G. Chambers, Mark Foulon, Helen Handfield-Jones, Steven M. Hankin, and Edward G. Michaels III, "The War for Talent," *McKinsey Quarterly* no. 3 (1998).

10. Alfred Rappaport, "How To Link Executive Pay With Performance," *Harvard Business Review,* March–April 1999, 93.

Chapter Three

1. Gary Hamel, *Leading the Revolution* (Boston: Harvard Business School Press, 2000), 25.

Chapter Four

1. Stephan Haeckel, *Adaptive Enterprise* (Boston: Harvard Business School Press, 1999), 40.

2. Adrian Poffley, *Financial Stewardship of Charities* (London: The Directory of Social Change, 2002), 152–153; <http://www.sightsavers.org>, (accessed 16 October 2002).

Chapter Five

1. John Kotter, *Leading Change* (Boston: Harvard Business School Press, 1996), 156.

Chapter Six

1. Margaret Wheatley, "Goodbye, Command and Control," *Leader to Leader* no. 5 (Summer 1997).

2. John Oliver, *The Team Enterprise Solution* (Cork, Ireland: Oak Tree Press, 2001), 208–209.

3. Oliver, *The Team Enterprise Solution,* 145.

4. Oliver, 194–195.

5. Oliver, 195.

6. Oliver, 191.

7. Oliver, 55–56.

8. Oliver, 56.

Chapter Seven

1. Charles Handy, "Balancing Corporate Power: A New Federalist Paper," *Harvard Business Review,* November–December 1992, 59–67.

2. Robert Simons, *Performance Measurement and Control Systems for Implementing Strategy* (Upper Saddle River, NJ: Prentice Hall, 2000), 281.

3. Sumantra Ghoshal and Christopher A. Bartlett, *The Individualized Corporation* (London: Heinemann, 1998), 311.

4. Ghoshal and Bartlett, *The Individualized Corporation,* 310.

Chapter Eight

1. Edgar Schein, *The Corporate Culture Survival Guide* (San Francisco: Jossey-Bass, 1999), 117–118.

2. John Oliver, *The Team Enterprise Solution* (Cork, Ireland: Oak Tree Press, 2001), 48.

3. Oliver, *The Team Enterprise Solution,* 96.

4. Oliver, 10.

5. Oliver, 11.

6. H. Thomas Johnson, "Reflections of a Recovering Management Accountant," Assessment for Learning Research Initiative conference, January 14–16, 1998; <http://www.sol-ne.org/com/ar98/index.html>, (accessed 29 January 2001).

7. Robert Slater, *Jack Welch and the GE Way* (New York: McGraw Hill, 1999), 90.

8. Oliver, *Team Enterprise Solution,* 232.

9. Schein, *Corporate Culture Survival Guide,* 143.

10. Peter Senge, *Rethinking the Future* (London: Nicholas Brealey Publishing, 1997), 140–141.

11. Arne Mårtensson, Handelsbanken Annual Report (2001), 3.

12. Lars Grönstedt, Handelsbanken Annual Report (2002).

Chapter Nine

1. Robert S. Kaplan and David P. Norton, *The Strategy-Focused Organization* (Boston: Harvard Business School Press, 2001), 14.

2. Quoted in Robert MacLuhan, "How CRM Impacts the Bottom Line," *Marketing,* 9 May 2002, 25.

3. Alfred Rappaport, "How To Link Executive Pay With Performance," *Harvard Business Review,* March–April 1999, 93.

4. Kaplan and Norton, *The Strategy-Focused Organization,* 16.

5. Report by QCi Assessment, quoted in Robert MaLuhan, "How CRM Impacts the Bottom Line," *Marketing Magazine* (UK), 9 May 2002, 25.

Chapter Ten

1. Peter M. Senge, "The Leader's New Work: Building Learning Organizations," *Sloan Management Review* 32, no. 1 (1990): 3.

2. Elizabeth G. Chambers, Mark Foulon, Helen Handfield-Jones, Steven M. Hankin, and Edward G. Michaels III, "The War for Talent," *McKinsey Quarterly* no. 3 (1998).

3. Tom Stewart, "Your Company's Most Valuable Asset: Intellectual Capital," *Fortune,* 3 October 1994, 32.

4. Joel Kurtzman, "An Interview with Gary Hamel," *Strategy & Business,* Fourth Quarter, 1997, 97.

5. Margaret Wheatley, *Leadership and the New Science* (San Francisco: Berret-Koehler Publishers, 1999), 107–108.

6. Richard Donkin, *Blood, Sweat, & Tears* (New York: Texere, 2001).

7. Donkin, *Blood, Sweat, & Tears,* 52.

Index

About the Authors

JEREMY HOPE is currently research director of the Beyond Budgeting Round Table (BBRT), an organization dedicated to helping firms improve their performance management processes. He began his career as a chartered accountant and has since had experience in venture capital and business management.

Hope is the author of a number of articles and books on performance management and associated leadership issues. His article on beyond budgeting with Robin Fraser won the prestigious International Federation of Accountants (IFAC) award for best management accounting article of 1998. He is coauthor (with Robin Fraser) of the article "Who Needs Budgets?" in *Harvard Business Review*. He is also coauthor (with his brother Tony Hope) of *Transforming the Bottom Line* (1995) and *Competing in the Third Wave* (1997), both published by Harvard Business School Press. He has given many keynote speeches at major conferences on performance management topics. He can be reached at jeremyhope@bbrt.org.

ROBIN FRASER is a management consultant, formerly a partner in the United Kingdom with Coopers & Lybrand (C&L) (until recently PricewaterhouseCoopers, and now IBM Business Consulting Services). He has specialized in business planning, performance improvement, and cost reduction, and worked with clients in all sectors. While with C&L, he led the development of Priority Base Budgeting (PBB) and headed the firm's Activity-Based Management (ABM) practice. He also represented C&L in CAM-I (Consortium for Advanced Manufacturing—International, Inc.), leading a research project into budgeting, and cochairing its Advanced Management Systems (AMS) program in Europe. Earlier in his career, he worked in Iran for seven years and was a partner in C&L's Tehran office. Prior to joining C&L, he completed a degree in chemical engineering, worked as an industrial engineer in RTZ and British Oxygen, and qualified as a management accountant.

For the past five years Fraser has co-led the beyond budgeting project with Jeremy Hope and is now leading the development of the BBRT internationally. He is a regular speaker on beyond budgeting at conferences, public courses, and in-company workshops. He can be reached at robinfraser@bbrt.org.